The Official Guide To
GOLDFISH
GOLDFISH SOCIETY OF AMERICA

T.F.H. Plaza • Third and Union Aves. • Neptune City, NJ 07753

Introduction

DEDICATION

The Goldfish Society of America was established to bring together people who enjoy the ages-old hobby of Goldfish Keeping. We would like to thank the farsighted men and women who took the time, and did the work, that made this Society possible. To those founding members, we dedicate this book.

Goldfish have brought more joy and frustration to the fish keeping hobby than probably any other fish. The misinformation, fables and the fact that some goldfish are extremely hardy, has usually caused this fish an untimely demise.

This book was written with the beginning goldfish hobbyist in mind and is far from complete. Using this book and a little common sense should help to keep your goldfish in a healthy and happy state for many years. The goldfish hobbyists, be they novice or expert, should never stop researching and studying their lovely pet. Society publications and goldfish books published by the pet industry are all sources of information, but the most up-to-date information on goldfish comes from corresponding with other hobbyists. The Goldfish Society of America has provided a forum to meet and correspond with people who enjoy goldfish for their beauty, their adaptability, their variety and the constant challenge to achieve perfection.

We hope this book will provide the beginning hobbyist with the basic tools for successful goldfish keeping. In this way we hope the beginner will avoid many of the pitfalls and misinformation that have led earlier hobbyists to give up in frustration.

A drawing of the old standard of a Deme Ranchu goldfish. One hundred years ago this fish was the rage of Japan.

2

General Care

Goldfish Housing

Goldfish are best kept in ponds and aquariums that have enough surface area to support the high oxygen demands of a goldfish. Aquariums of the long and low type will hold more fish than a tall narrow aquarium of the same gallonage.

Goldfish bowls are not a good home for goldfish, as they lack enough surface area to maintain a fish for any length of time. If you must use a goldfish bowl then only partially fill it to the widest part of the bowl to achieve maximum surface area . . . and also to help prevent your goldfish from jumping out of it.

Ponds are wonderful for goldfish. They should be deep enough and contain enough water to keep rapid temperature variations from happening. If the pond is outside, shade must be provided for at least part of the day to control algae and to give the fish a break from the sunshine. Constant partial shade is best.

Temporary goldfish tanks can be made from children's wading pools, large plastic bowls, plastic cat litter boxes, five-gallon buckets and many other plastic items. Plastic sheeting can be used to line heavy cardboard boxes, wood frames and holes dug in the ground to form permanent and/or

Goldfish are hardy animals and if the principles of aeration, cleanliness and not overcrowding are observed, goldfish can be kept in a clean wooden tub or an ornate goldfish pool (below).

temporary goldfish quarters.

As you can see, goldfish can be kept in just about any non-toxic container that will hold water. But those containers with a lot of surface area are the better choices for goldfish housing. More surface area equals more inches of goldfish that can safely be maintained in a container. The rule of thumb in an unfiltered, unaerated container is *30 square inches of surface area to every inch of goldfish body*.

If the goldfish container is filtered, then the container can hold slightly more goldfish, but be on the safe side and don't push it too much, as a power failure could wipe out your whole collection of goldfish. A tank or pond that is slightly undercrowded will be much less work and have fewer problems than a slightly overcrowded one.

Suggested designs for outside goldfish ponds. Drawings by John R. Quinn.

Filters

There are two basic types of water filtration systems used in the goldfish hobby. These are mechanical and biological filtration.

Mechanical filtration uses a material to physically remove particulate matter from the water, and many may use carbon or charcoal to remove toxic gases before returning the water to the tank or pond. Mechanical filters come in power models that use water pumps to move a great deal of water in and out of the filter, and air operated models that move the water much more slowly through

water output

water intake

A typical high quality power filter which may be available through your local petshop. This is an excerpt from *Tropical Fish Hobbyist* Magazine.

Excerpts from advertisements appearing in *Tropical Fish Hobbyist* Magazine, showing different types and sizes of aquarium power filters which work from outside the tank.

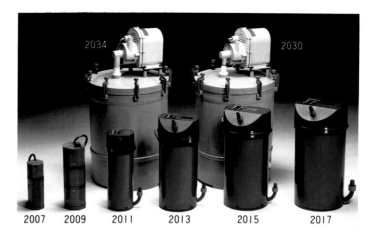

The name brand products illustrated or mentioned in this book are not endorsed either by the Goldfish Society of America or the publishers.

the filter. Either type of filter is acceptable with goldfish and works well. High volume power filters should be adjusted to prevent strong water currents in the tank or pond, for goldfish don't do well in heavy currents. Air-operated filters should be the type that use an airstone, as these move a great deal more water through the filter.

Biological filtration is usually associated with the undergravel filter, although canister and power filters can be adapted to biological filtration methods. Undergravel filters filter the water by trapping the particulate waste in the bottom gravel where nitrifying and other bacteria can break it down into less toxic substances.

Undergravel filters are now commonly operated by the use of a powerhead which increases the circulation of water through the gravel many times over. Using a powerhead on an undergravel filter increases the efficiency of the gravel/bacteria filter, which means a large tank can be totally filtered with an undergravel filter.

If your undergravel filter is airstone-operated then it might be helpful to use some mechanical filtration in conjunction with it. A filtration system that uses both mechanical and biological filtration is the best method for goldfish and results in crystal-clear, clean water for your fish to live in.

A portable easy-to-clean

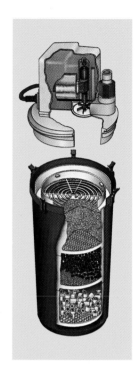

pond or large tank filter can be made by using a cat litter box, 12″ × 12″ undergravel filter plate, gravel and a large powerhead. These portable undergravel filters are easy to clean and do a very good job in filtering a large amount of water.

Another type of filter that is smaller than the above, therefore easier to use in a small tank, is made by using a shallow plastic bowl with a goldfish bowl undergravel filter in it. This works well in a fry tank or hospital tank. The gravel size should be adjusted to the size of the fish that are in the tank, i.e., small gravel for fry and coarse for adult goldfish.

Biological filters take two to four weeks to reach full

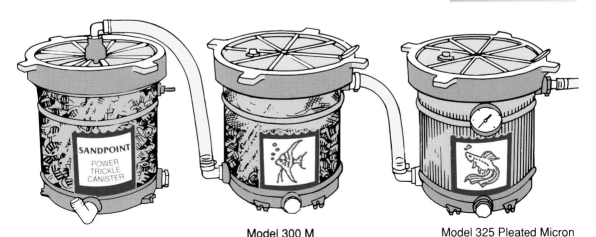

Model 310 Power Trickle Canister

Model 300 M Chemical Canister

Model 325 Pleated Micron Cartridge Canister

LG 300
for up to 300 gallons

RAINBOW LIFEGARD

RAINBOW LIFEGARD

LIFEGARD® PRE-FILTER
with "no siphon break" and exclusive flow control valve for silent operation.

LG 150
for up to 150 gallons

efficiency, as the bacteria take time to become established. So give your undergravel filters time to adjust and add fish slowly in a tank that is filtered biologically. As mentioned earlier, the best filtration system for goldfish combines both the mechanical and biological methods, but either system used alone, if not overworked, will work well.

Setting up the Goldfish Tank

Goldfish do not demand fancy quarters. A container with lots of surface area, good water and a filter is about all that is needed. But most of us like to have our tanks dressed up just a bit. So gravel, plants, rocks, a light source, and a decorative back are all among the items that are purchased. In setting up the aquarium, remember to wash everything very well. Use warm salt water; do not use

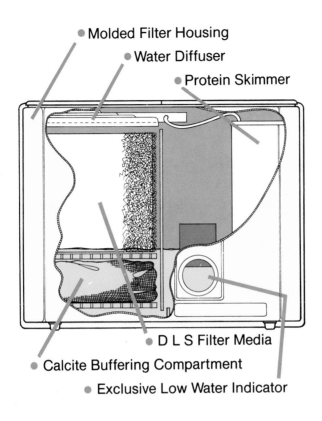

- Molded Filter Housing
- Water Diffuser
- Protein Skimmer
- D L S Filter Media
- Calcite Buffering Compartment
- Exclusive Low Water Indicator

These excerpts from advertisements in *Tropical Fish Hobbyist* Magazine show the types and functions of filters available at aquarium speciality stores.

There are wonderful outside power filters, so dependable that they even function perfectly when turned upside down!

cleansers, bleach, soap, etc., as these can be harmful to goldfish if not thoroughly rinsed out. The gravel should be rinsed in a bucket to remove any dust and dirt which will cloud the aquarium's water. Do not use sea shells or ornaments with holes that can trap waste materials. Avoid all objects with sharp edges as they can damage scales, eye growths and fins.

Choose a location for your tank that will be out of the way, but easily viewed. Make sure the floor is strong enough to hold the tank, as the tank, gravel and water will become very heavy when placed all together. Try to locate it away from a window or any heat source to prevent sunlight, or an artificial heat source, from heating the water to dangerous levels.

Goldfish do not demand or even like a bright light. A room that is light enough to read in is usually sufficiently lit to keep goldfish in an

unlighted tank. But, if you want a tank with a light, then choose a reflector with a fluorescent light, as this is a much cooler light and will not overheat the water as

Goldfish tanks come in all sizes and shapes. Most are fitted with a light and a built-in cover, otherwise you can use a normal lamp. Keep the light away from the tank so it doesn't overheat the water.

much as other methods.

Before adding fish to the aquarium, the water should be treated with a chlorine neutralizer and allowed to sit at least overnight. In fact, if the tank can sit for a week without fish, you will be much further ahead, as this gives everything in the tank a chance to stabilize. *And remember:* add fish slowly to a new aquarium to allow the aquarium time to become biologically established.

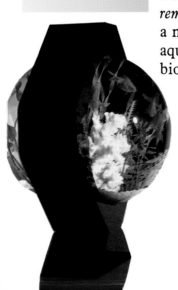

Your child can set up the goldfish tank by herself. You should just be sure that the tank is set on a sturdy stand and that the gravel, rocks, and other addenda are safe for aquarium fishes. Photo by Dr. Herbert R. Axelrod.

Aquarium Bologna (Italy) manufactures this beautiful goldfish aquarium.

Purchasing Goldfish

When you enter a pet shop on a goldfish hunting trip, do so with caution. Because of the increased demand for fancy goldfish and lack of knowledge of some pet shop personnel you will find a lot of mislabeled, poor quality and over-priced goldfish at those shops that have very little experience with goldfish. But if you look long and hard, chances are you'll run across a pet shop owner who actually knows what he is talking about and this is usually a good place to buy your goldfish.

Wherever you buy your goldfish, look for healthy active goldfish with no outward signs of disease. Avoid those with torn fins, missing scales (a few missing scales are o.k.), fungus, cloudy eyes, clamped fins, parasite infections such as ich, fish lice, anchorworm, etc., rapid breathing, and any other abnormality. Goldfish who lack vigor or spend their time shyly hiding are poor prospects and should be avoided.

Since goldfish come in various breeds, you should at least have a basic understanding of some of the different breed standards. Understanding these standards is very helpful in buying mature goldfish as breed characteristics should be well developed in mature fish. Immature goldfish are usually fairly difficult to select for potential breed characteristics development, as it takes many breeds six months to one year to show potential for them.

Breeds such as Orandas, Lionheads, Ranchus, Ryukins, and other shortbodied fish take as long as one year to develop the appropriate body shape for that breed. In selecting young goldfish for this feature, select those that are not too long in body, that have a gentle curve along the back and show a full round belly. All young goldfish will seem too long for their breed, but with good food high in carbohydrates, they can develop into beautiful full-bodied fish.

Breeds with head growth should show signs of developing this characteristic when they are two to three inches long. This early growth is easiest seen on the top of the head, and there should be a slight raised area

Above: A red Ranchu with a nicely proportioned head, body and tail. Photo by Fred Rosenzweig. Left: A head-on view of a Telescope-eyed goldfish. Photo by Burkhard Kahl.

Facing page: A back view of a nice red-capped Oranda. Photo by Fred Rosenzweig. Right: A common Comet goldfish with a long single tailfin. Photo by Michael Gilroy. Below: An outside filter of modern design and efficiency.

in the region where the head meets the body along the back. The easiest way to select young fish for potential head growth is to look *down* at the fish and examine the shape of the head. The head of an Oranda, Lionhead or Ranchu should be broad between the eyes and should end at the mouth in a blunt almost squared-off fashion. Fish with this broad square head will usually (but not always) develop a good head growth, if properly cared for and fed the proper diet.

Goldfish that develop head growths should be fed a diet higher in protein than would normally be fed to goldfish. Live or frozen red worms are an excellent source of

protein, as are Bloodworms, Daphnia, Mosquito larvae and other live or frozen animal protein foods.

When selecting any breed of goldfish, look for well developed and symmetrical finnage. All the fins should be there (except for the dorsal in dorsalless breeds) and they should not have any bent or broken fins.

Doubletailed breeds should have two tail fins that are separated from each other completely (exceptions: Ranchus, Lionheads and Pompons). It is a rare fish that has this complete division as most are partially or wholly joined at the top (web tailed). All double-tailed breeds should have four lobes to the tail. In

Facing page: This red-cap Oranda is very poor quality. The dorsal and other fins are too short, though the head growth is acceptable. The body should be rounder and deeper. The fish is in poor health with missing scales and slightly bloody fins. Photo by Michael Gilroy.

some cases tripod-tailed (three lobes) goldfish will escape the culler's net and be offered for sale. A fish has a tripod tail if it has two bottom tail fin lobes attached to a single top lobe.

All double-tailed breeds have two anal fins. These double anals should be the same size and shape. In short-tailed breeds, the anal fins should be short with the opposite being true in long-tailed breeds. In dorsalless breeds, look for smooth backs with no dorsal spikes or bumps.

Goldfish colors should be bright, dense, and even over the entire body.

In calico goldfish black, red, and blue are the colors to look for, but you may have to settle for fish with some yellow, orange, brown, and slate gray. In calico fish, you will also have scales that are very reflective and those that are transparent. A good balance between these two types of scales should be looked for with the transparent scales in the

This is a very poor Lionhead with a bad back and little if any head growth. Photo by Burkhard Kahl.

majority. The reason for more transparent scales is that they allow for a purer blue to be seen as the blue color (black pigment) comes from beneath the scales.

Since there are so few show quality goldfish available, you will find very few (if any) who meet all the standards for a breed. But don't let this stop you as a fish with a few minor flaws can still be, and probably will be, a gorgeous fish. Since goldfish improve with age, give your goldfish one or two years to develop before you judge them too harshly.

Quarantine

All newly purchased fish should be isolated from your other fish until they have proven they are free of disease and parasites. Usually 10 to 14 days is considered enough time for trouble to appear.

Goldfish bought on the retail market (and some hobbyist-bred fish) have been exposed to some pretty adverse conditions and more diseases than you would find in a doctor's waiting room. Quarantining your newly purchased fish is an act of kindness as it gives the new fish time to adjust and build

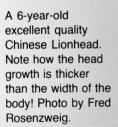

A 6-year-old excellent quality Chinese Lionhead. Note how the head growth is thicker than the width of the body! Photo by Fred Rosenzweig.

A rare peach-colored Pearlscale with excellent scaling. This fish took first prize at an American show. Photo by Fred Rosenzweig.

its strength, without being hassled by other fish.

Quarantining quarters need not be large or elaborate for a single fish. A 5 gallon bucket, styrofoam ice chest, or a heavy cardboard box lined with plastic sheeting all make good quarantine tanks if placed in an area of stable temperature. A large box filter will handle the water filtration and circulation in these small temporary tanks.

While you have your goldfish in isolation, you should treat for parasites such as Gill Flukes, Anchor Worm and Fish Lice. Parasites are a constant but easily controlled problem, and can be treated easily and cheaply while the fish is in quarantine.

Feeding

Goldfish will eat just about anything! This true statement means that goldfish are perhaps one of the easiest fish to feed.

A goldfish food high in carbohydrates (plant food), with a moderate amount of protein (15% – 30%) and low in fat will keep your goldfish healthy and active for years. As in all animal feeding (people, too) a variety of food is important to assure a

Right: A can of goldfish food in flake form. Goldfish foods are formulated in a number of different forms such as dried, frozen, and freeze-dried and in different consistencies such as flakes, granules, and pellets, so goldfish keepers have a wide variety to choose from. Below: A Calico Butterfly Telescope with fair color and weak finnage. Photo by Burkhard Kahl.

balanced diet. If you feed dry food, you should feed two or three different kinds to give variety to the goldfish's diet. Pelleted or ground foods of the appropriate sizes are a better type of food than flake foods.

Older goldfish gulp a lot of air when feeding from the surface, which if swallowed can leave you with a floating fish. This floating condition usually will go away in a day or two but until it does, the fish is under a great deal of harmful stress.

It might be wise to pre-soak your dry food as goldfish who eat a lot of unsoaked dry food very quickly can have digestive problems. This digestive problem (constipation) is caused by the food absorbing water in the intestine, leaving the fish with an impacted intestine. Another way around this problem is to feed small amounts at each feeding and to increase the number of feedings to assure they get enough to eat.

Live foods or fresh frozen foods such as Daphnia, Brine shrimp, Redworms, Blood worms, Mosquito larvae, wingless Fruitflies, etc., should be fed to goldfish as often as possible. Although the fish can be fed dry food for years with no adverse effects, an occasional feeding of live or fresh frozen food is a proven benefit.

Overfeeding of goldfish is probably one of the leading causes of death in older specimens. Since goldfish are always hungry, it's really very easy to overfeed them. A once-a-day feeding is usually enough to keep the average pampered goldfish happy. Pond goldfish, if allowed to go through a period of cold water hibernation, should be fed heavier than tank raised fish, to allow them to build a food reserve. If a goldfish does not go through a yearly hibernation, then keep the feeding schedule light to prevent obese goldfish.

A pair of high quality brocaded (random glitter scales) calico Oranda goldfish. Photo by Fred Rosenzweig.

Water Quality

Goldfish thrive in just about any water that is good enough to drink. A pH of 6.8 to 7.6 is ideal, although they can live in water with a pH as high as 8.0 very easily. Moderately hard water is beneficial to goldfish, although they can live in very soft to very hard water just as well.

Goldfish are very susceptible to ammonia poisoning. Ammonia can burn the gills, body, and fins as well as destroy the kidneys and circulatory system and is especially harmful if the pH is over 7.2. Some water supplies are treated with chloramines (chlorine x ammonia) and if this chemical is not eliminated, your fish will be harmed or killed. Check with your pet shops for a chemical treatment to remove chloramines if the water in

Ammonia is a by-product of organic waste which, if properly treated, becomes a nitrate fertilizer for aquatic plants.

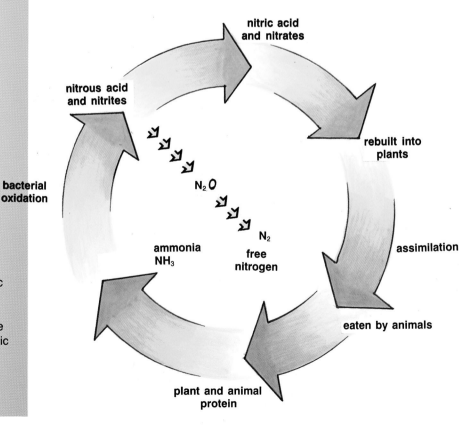

This is a lovely quality, young nacreous Veiltail goldfish with a classic dorsal and caudal fin. Photo by Burkhard Kahl.

our area is treated with it.

Fresh water from the tap in most areas needs to be treated to neutralize the chlorine. It should also be allowed to sit for several hours before being used, to allow the compressed gases to dissipate.

Water Changes

For maintaining good health, water changes are one of the most important things the goldfish hobbyist can do. Even with a good filtration system, harmful gases and substances will build up in the water. Ammonia, nitrites and nitrates are all very harmful to goldfish and the best way to keep these harmful chemicals at low levels is to regularly change the water.

Depending on the tank or pond's population, temperature, filtration system, organic waste build-ups, type and amount of food being fed, a 10% to 50% partial water change is recommended every week. The key phrase for water

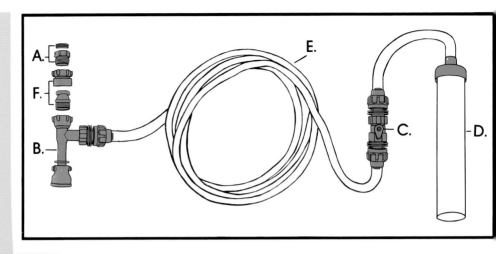

Petshops have many gadgets which make goldfish-keeping easier. The water-changer shown above and the water conditioner Amquel are just two of the products which may be available.

A. **TWO PIECE FAUCET ADAPTOR:**
Use as needed to attach Pump (B) to any standard faucet.

B. **FAUCET PUMP:**
Creates strong suction to clean. Has reverse flow feature for easy refilling.

C. **OPEN/CLOSE SWITCH:**
Manually controls removal of waste and refilling with clean fresh water.

D. **CLEAR GRAVEL TUBE:**
Goes into the gravel for cleaning and into the tank for refilling.

E. **FDA-APPROVED, NON-TOXIC CLEAR, FLEXIBLE TUBING:**
Carries water to and from the tank.

F. **SNAP CONNECTOR (OPTIONAL):**
Makes attaching the pump to the faucet a "snap".

changes is *"frequent partial water changes."*

If you have trouble keeping goldfish alive for any length of time, poor water quality should be the first area you should check. Once the hobbyist realizes the importance of water changes and does them regularly, 90% of the troubles will disappear. All replacement water should be treated for chlorine, chloramines and compressed gases. It is a good idea to buy several 5-gallon buckets and keep some full of aged water for that weekly water change.

Temperatures

Goldfish come from the temperate climate region of the world. They are not happy in water that is held at a constant high level. They are happiest with temperatures in the 60° to 70° F. range. This is the ideal feeding and growing temperature, and if possible the temperature should be maintained at this level for most of the year.

and gulp air, then the hobbyist should increase water circulation, reduce the number of fish in the container or find some way to keep the water temperature from rising. Goldfish can handle 90° F. water temperatures *IF* their

This is a very poor quality Chinese Lionhead with small Pompons. The head growth is weak, the back is uneven and the caudal peduncle is poor. The angle of the fins is terrible. Photo by Burkhard Kahl.

Temperatures above 70° F. mean less oxygen in the water so a careful watch should be made during the hottest part of the day for oxygen starvation. If your goldfish come to the surface

container is uncrowded and well circulated.

Temperatures below 60° F. mean the goldfish will have less of an appetite as the temperature lowers. Although goldfish will eat even in water covered by ice, most hobbyists will stop feeding when the temperature drops below 40° F. A careful watch needs to be kept on your goldfish at this time to make sure they are eating what you are feeding. Overfeeding at this time can cause water pollution which can cause diseases or ammonia poisoning.

Plants

For the Aquarium: Only the tough water plants can be successfully kept with goldfish, as they eat plants.

Good plants to use with goldfish are: Amazon swords, Cryptocorynes, giant Vallisneria, all type of Sagittarias, Banana plants, and if you have a good bright light, some of the Dwarf Tropical water lilies are good.

For the Pond: Water lilies are by far the best pond plants as they provide shade and shelter for your goldfish. Because plants grow so fast in the outside sunlit pond, many of the softer plants can be grown in the pond. Besides all the plants listed for aquariums, plants like

A very old and almost extinct breed is the Phoenix Calico. It is a long-tailed, thin-bodied Lionhead with a dusting of head growth. Photo by Fred Rosenzweig.

Anacharis and Myriophyllum can be grown in the pond. Water lettuce and water hyacinths are excellent pond plants and their long trailing roots make great spawning medium for goldfish.

Plants as Food: Green plants are a great food source for adult goldfish. Duckweed, Water Sprite, Anacharis, some algae and some garden greens partially cooked to tenderize them all are very good foods for goldfish.

Gravel

The gravel used with goldfish should be medium coarse and smooth. Goldfish do a lot of browsing on the bottom and if sharp gravel is used it could damage their mouth. By using a medium coarse gravel, the underwater excavating that goldfish seem to take such great pleasure in doing will be lessened.

Goldfish from time to time will get a piece of gravel lodged in their mouth. If the fish does not show signs of distress, allow it several hours to dislodge it itself. If the fish is unable to breathe, hold it in a head-down position, gently press in on the sides of the lips to open the mouth to its maximum and then with the tip of the forefinger of your other hand

Poor quality short-tailed Pearlscale goldfish. The dorsal is very weak and the body should be rounder and deeper. This is pure junk as a Pearlscale. Photo by Michael Gilroy.

27

*Myriophyllum
brasiliense.* Photo by
R. Zukal.

gently press in on the throat behind the stone and work it forward to lift the stone up and out of the mouth. Relief usually is immediate and the fish should show no ill effect from its ordeal. However, a fish that will have this happen once will quite often have it happen again and should be watched or the gravel size in the tank changed.

Tank, Gravel, and Filter Cleaning

Once or twice a year the goldfish tank should be emptied and thoroughly cleaned. The tank should be drained, all the gravel, plants, fish (of course) removed, and thoroughly washed with fresh water (not the fish). Remove all mineral deposits with a razor blade or sponge.

The gravel can be cleaned by rinsing it in a bucket or by placing the gravel in a colander and running cool water through it. If the gravel smells alright there is no reason to sun dry it or replace it. If it has gone foul (black) then replace it or allow it to dry in the sun 10 to 14 days.

The mechanical filters

should not be cleaned at the time of a complete tank break down. By using an established filter in a freshly set up tank, the aquarium will settle down (clear up) faster and be safer for your goldfish. To clean a filter just rinse with clean water and set it back up.

If you cannot tear your tank down completely then your local fish shop has some pretty handy equipment that will do a pretty good job of cleaning the gravel, tank, and filter.

Another hint in tank cleaning is never change the water and clean your filter on the same day. Because of the reduction of the beneficial bacteria when the water is changed and the filters are cleaned, you could experience an increase of ammonia which is very harmful to goldfish. Change the water first and clean the filter later.

Companions for Goldfish

The best companions for goldfish are other goldfish. But even this statement is only partially true. Occasionally one will find an aggressive goldfish that will badger its tank mates. Newly

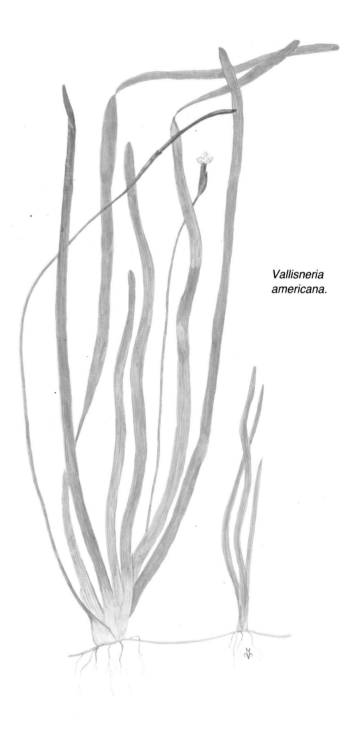

Vallisneria americana.

Top view of a fixed-eyed Celestial. Photo by Michael Gilroy.

added fish are the usual victims and the aggressor may have to be removed for a few days until the newcomer is "at home" in its new quarters.

Singletailed and doubletailed goldfish should not be kept together because the faster singletailed fish will consume the major amount of the food. For the same reason those breeds with impaired vision such as Telescopes, Bubble-eyes, and Celestials should not be forced to compete with the other breeds for their share of the food. Brown goldfish of any breed are frequently found to be much more energetic and aggressive to their tank mates, especially if their tank mates happen to be of the long finned or impaired vision varieties. It

A Broadtail Telescope with very delicate finnage. The blood in the veins of the fish may be due to excess heavy metals or ammonia. Photo by Fred Rosenzweig.

is desirable whenever possible to keep the various "types" of goldfish by themselves but harmonious tanks of mixed "types" are the most commonly found among novices and as long as they are all singletailed or all doubletailed, there is a good chance the harmony will continue for years.

Never keep tropical fish and goldfish together as their diets and temperature requirements are not compatible. Never put native fresh water fish such as Perch, Bream, Gambusia, etc., with goldfish as the fancy breeds of goldfish are no match for the native fish and seldom survive. Above all, never put cold water Catfish with goldfish. They love to suck the eyes out of goldfish and sooner or later will attack and kill the goldfish who may still be larger than they are.

Breeding

Why?

Why does someone go to the trouble, the time and effort to spawn, hatch, and raise goldfish? The answer to that question is as varied as the number of people who keep and propagate goldfish.

For some, it is the challenge of producing and having the best. For others, it is the challenge of creating a goldfish breed that is not available or for that matter, even in existence, while for others it is the pride of maintaining and improving a line of goldfish whose ancestry goes back for many generations. No matter what the reason, goldfish can and do provide the challenge to keep your interest alive, and in turn, will give you a fish whose beauty and variety are unmatched by any other fish.

You might be thinking that's all well and good but why not just walk down to the pet shop and buy one of these wonderful fish? Goldfish are just a little bit funny when it comes to the production of high quality

A closeup of a Hamanishiki. This looks like a Pearlscaled Oranda, except that the head growth is in 2 uniform bumps on the head. Photo by Fred Rosenzweig.

A beautiful long-finned Fringetail with only a dusting for a head growth. Photo by Fred Rosenzweig.

fish. They have the habit of reverting back to their ancestral form, i.e., olive green colored, long bodied, single finned crucian carp. For the prospective purchaser of a high quality goldfish, this reversion to ancestral type makes the purchase of a high quality goldfish next to impossible.

In each spawn of goldfish you will find young fry that are deformed, weak, poorly colored, lacking fins, having unwanted fins, non-standard body shapes, poorly shaped fins, improper head, and dozens of other defects that make them unsuitable. In some breeds, the percentage of these defective fish may be as little as 1%, while in other breeds which carry multiple breed characteristics, it may be as high as 99.9%. In this latter group, it means that only one or two fish in each spawn will prove to be worthy of its breed standard.

Now you can see why it is seldom possible to buy a high quality goldfish or some of the rare, or even semi-rare breeds of goldfish. In fact it may take years of searching just to find a halfway decent pair of these rare breeds, so that you can start on the long road of linebreeding to

33

Wild type goldfish, *Carassius auratus.*

improve your chosen breed.

Why breed goldfish? The reasons are as many as the number of people who do. But the pleasure and pride that raising high quality goldfish can bring is enough to have made the goldfish the oldest domesticated fish in the world.

Tank Size
Spawning. To determine the right size for a spawning tank, you must keep three items in mind, namely the number of fish used in spawning, the breed being spawned, and the size of the spawners.

In spawning goldfish, there are many ways to match your fish for spawning. For convenience and to simplify these methods, let's classify them in three groups: pairs, trios and multiples (flock method).

Breeding in a one-pair spawning tank takes the least room of any method. One male and one female, needless to say, is all that you need. The tank ideally should be at least 30 gallons in size and of the long and low type. Of course goldfish have spawned, and will continue to spawn, in smaller tanks, but for the safety of the female, she should be given some running room to escape the male(s) if she needs to.

The trio method consists of two males and one female. This method takes only just a bit more room than the pair method. Usually for most breeds of goldfish of small to medium sizes a 30 gallon long and low aquarium will do nicely.

The flock method is a method that uses multiple males with multiple females. The males should always outnumber the females with two-to-one male to female ratio being adequate but not necessary. This type of spawning will necessitate a much larger tank than the first two methods and is easier when using a breeding pond. The flock method has proven to be very helpful in improving the quality of a breed faster by increasing the chances for a proper match between your spawners. This method works best when used with a linebred strain of goldfish because of the close genetic background

Closely related to the goldfish, *Carassius auratus*, is this very rare *Carassius carassius*. They are distinguishable from goldfish by the spot on the caudal peduncle of the younger fish. Photo by Stanislas Frank.

these fish share. For outcrossing or developmental crossing, the pair and trio method is easier to control.

When choosing the right size spawning tank although this is a convenience rather than a necessity.

Also, take into consideration the size of your spawners. You might very

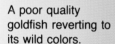

A poor quality goldfish reverting to its wild colors.

remember the rule of *"30 square inches to every inch of fish."* If you can, you should try to double this to give your spawners room to roam.

Some breeds, such as the singlefinned group, are more active in the spawning chase than the heavy-bodied doubletailed breeds. Singletailed and some of the more active doubletailed breeds should be given more room in their spawning tank

successfully spawn a pair of one-year-old Orandas in a 15 gallon tank, but a four-year-old pair of nine inch Orandas would not have enough room to turn around in that same tank. Once again, remember the *"rule of thirty and double it,"* and increase that tank space as the fish grow larger.

Fertility is one last item that might be worth considering when determining the size of your spawning tank. It has been found that when a smaller tank is used in spawning, the fertility of the spawn will increase. This should be a consideration only when breeding a fish that has a low fertility or hatch rate, and then only if we must use a fish of low fertility. The object of any breeding program should be never to use weak or unproductive fish unless it is absolutely necessary.

The Hatchery and Fry Tanks. The first and only concrete rule in raising goldfish fry is *"don't overcrowd."* Sounds easy, right? Well, it's not! It's pretty hard to judge just how much room those itty bitty fry need. So starting with the eggs and working up, we will try to give guidelines for you to work from. We will try to err on the uncrowded side, when a recommendation is made, and you will find that if you err this way, both with fry and adults, your troubles will be few.

When it comes to tank hatching of goldfish eggs, there are two basic methods. The first is to leave the eggs in the spawning tank. This method insures that all of the eggs spawned will have a chance to hatch. The

A common Comet goldfish. The colors are changing and the fish will eventually be all orange. Photo by A. Roth.

A very poor quality short-tailed Pearlscale. Photo by A. Roth.

spawning tank, if you have followed the previous guidelines, will be large enough to hatch the eggs and raise the fry to the first culling, at the age of 10 feeding days old.

The second method is to

This is a poor quality bronze Oranda. Its finnage is of poor quality, the head growth is relatively minute and the body is uneven. Photo by Dr. Harry Grier of a Champion goldfish bred in Florida by the Florida Tropical Fish Farmer's Association. In most cases, the farmers themselves are the judges of this show.

remove the spawn with the spawning medium to a hatchery tank. This method will leave some eggs behind that are stuck to the tank, filter, etc. The benefit of this method is that the eggs can be divided into smaller tanks and the water in these tanks will be cleaner. The benefit of using more than one smaller tank is twofold. First, by having the fry in more than a single tank, it protects the spawn from being wiped out by disease. If you had a problem in one tank (disease, parasites) and you were careful not to contaminate your other tanks, you would be able to save at least part of the spawn.

Another plus for removing the eggs to a hatchery tank is that the water is cleaner. In a spawning tank, the eggs are exposed to a higher pollution level due to the presence of waste from the adult spawners and a lot of dying sperm. These two pollution sources cause the ammonia levels to be much higher in the spawning tank than it is in the hatchery tank. The only problem is that the two tanks (spawning and hatchery) should be filled with water from the same source at the same time. This prevents the eggs from being exposed to a great change in water quality (pH, hardness, composition). A hatchery tank of 20 gallons (long and low) will comfortably hold 500 to 750 eggs of newly hatched fry.

For the first 10 feeding days of a fry's life, the fry can live and grow quite happily in a somewhat crowded tank. This keeps them close to their food and with frequent water changes (daily), good filtration and aeration, they will grow very quickly. During the first 10 feeding days of their life, a good guide as to the fry density of a tank is 500 to a 20 gallon long and low tank (approximately 12″ x 30″ surface).

After the first culling, at 10 feeding days of age, the fry in each tank need to be split into two or more tanks if you have more than 50% of the fry left after culling. After the first culling, we start to use the surface area to determine the number of fry that can be maintained in a tank. When the fry are 10 feeding days old, it is safe to keep them at a density of 100 fry to 144 square inches of

This beautiful Ryukin may have some problems as its fins seem to be showing signs of blood. Usually this is due to excessive ammonia or nitrites in the water.

A nice quality blue-scale Oranda with a nice balance of head growth compared with its body and fins. It is full hooded and has no brown patches, which are frequent faults of blue-scaled fish. Photo by Burkhard Kahl.

surface area (12″ x 12″).

After the first culling and thinning (or spreading out) of the fry, every effort should be made either to cull the fry weekly or to give them bigger or more tanks. When the fry are four feeding weeks old, they should be maintained at a surface area density of 30 fry to 144 square inches of surface area. This culling and thinning should continue until at the age of eight weeks the fry should be maintained in the tank at the same rate as adult goldfish, i.e., 30 square inches to one inch of fish.

Remember, it is far safer to err in the direction of fewer fry than more fry. If you do not cull and keep the tank populations low, then disease and stress will do it for you. So why not become an active culler and raise only the best fry in a spawn, rather than those who have been the lucky survivors?

This white Oranda has a head growth that has encompassed the entire head region. Photo by Fred Rosenzweig.

Supplies

Spawning Tank: One 30 gallon or larger for each spawning group. The tank should be of the long and low type to increase the overall surface area. Water depth of 6–9 inches.

Hatchery or Fry Tank: Two or more 20 gallon or larger tanks for each spawn. Tanks should be of the long and low type to insure enough surface area. Water depth of 6–9 inches for the first four weeks.

Spawning Medium: Four to six 12 inch strands of a commercial spawning grass, tied in a group, and/or two to six homemade yarn and cork spawning mops. Natural plants such as Anacharis, Cabomba, Myriophyllum, Water Lettuce, Water Hyacinths, etc., loosely tied in large bunches.

Filters: (See Filters) Two sponge filters or two box filters for each hatchery tank. Two large box filters, power filter and/or undergravel filter in the spawning tank. Remove unmodified box filters when eggs start to hatch.

Syphons: One ½ inch clear flexible hose with a 12 inch ridged plastic tube inserted in the end. This large syphon is used for quick water changes and should have a sponge or filter floss attached to the end of the rigid tube to prevent syphoning any of the fry out of the tank. Also one airline tubing syphon with a 16 inch rigid plastic tube inserted in the end. This small syphon is used to slowly syphon the waste from the bottom of the tank while the fry are very small.

Buckets: Buckets of various sizes (one to five gallon) are useful for water changes, water ageing, culling and tank cleaning.

Nets: Although large adult goldfish can be caught with a net, it is safer for the fish's scales and fins if they are caught using your hands. A series of small nets for goldfish over eight weeks old are handy when moving large numbers of fish. A culling net can be made by removing the cloth screen from a commercial brine shrimp net or other small net and replacing it with a piece of nylon stocking stretched tight across the frame. Bend the net at a 45° angle to the

This blue-scale Oranda is losing color and a few scales (accidentally, of course). Some blue-scales eventually turn white.

Goldfish should not be lifted out of the water in a net as it may tear off their scales. Capture the fish in the net if you are unable to catch him with your hands. Bring the net to the surface then use a small globe to transfer the goldfish.

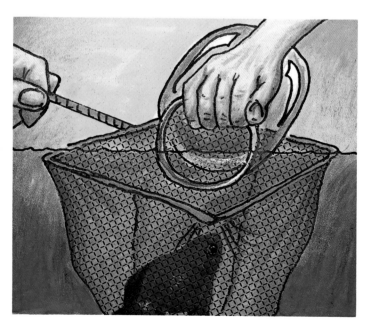

handle. It is recommended when moving fry under eight weeks old to scoop them up with a cup or a kitchen baster to prevent damaging the very tender fry.

Kitchen Baster: Used to catch very small fry.

Large White Plastic Bowls: Useful in culling fry.

Tea Cup: Used to catch small fry.

Fry Food Raising Equipment: (See Fry Foods) Bottles, jugs, air pumps, strainers, nets, buckets, tanks, and many more items might be needed, depending on the fry foods you feed.

Filters

The filtering of a spawning tank is very similar to the filtering of any other tank that houses large adult goldfish. If the spawning tank is to be used as a temporary spawning tank and the spawners are just temporary residents, then two large quilt-batting wrapped box filters will do a good job. In these temporary spawning tanks the spawners need not be fed, if they spawn within the first three days they are in the spawning tank. This helps reduce the waste matter in the tank and is very beneficial if the eggs are to be left in the tank to hatch.

Filtering the hatchery tank takes a little more study and care. With the exception of the sponge filter and the undergravel filter, no unmodified commercial filter will work with small fry due to the danger of drawing the fry into the filter, which will usually kill them. But with a little modifying, many commercial filters, be they air-operated or power, can work very well in all but the newly hatched fry tank.

For fry that have just hatched to 10 feeding days of age, a sponge filter or a box filter that has been wrapped in quilt-batting is all the filtration that is needed. Of the two types, sponge or box, the box filter filled with filter carbon and wrapped with quilt-batting will filter more water per hour, that is, if it is of the bubble-up type (airstone operated). In either case, both filters should have been in use for at least two weeks before being placed in the fry tank, to allow the establishment of beneficial bacteria. These beneficial bacteria will help reduce harmful pollutants such as ammonia and nitrites which are deadly to all goldfish.

As the fry get older and larger, the hatchery tank needs increased filtration. This can be accomplished at first by adding more sponge filters or quilt-batting wrapped box filters. But as the fry start to put on their rapid growth (usually at 4 weeks) their food consumption and waste start to skyrocket. At this time a modified power filter with a power intake is a handy tool. By wrapping the intake tube with quilt-batting or inserting the tube into a coarse sponge, the filter will operate fairly well without the danger of sucking the fry into it.

Another option at this time is to transfer large fry into a tank that has an established, but clean, undergravel filter in operation. Although an undergravel filter will give good results by itself, some mechanical filtration might be necessary. The big disadvantage of the undergravel filter is that the fry won't be able to pick up food that has settled on the bottom of the tank as easily as in a bare bottomed tank. Depending on the type of

A nicely developed red and white Oranda with a good, full hood and very deep body and fair finnage. Photo by Burkhard Kahl.

food you are feeding your older fry, (live, dry, paste) this may or may not be a problem.

Some caution should be exercised in controlling the currents created by the filter's exhaust. The fry should find at least one area in the tank that is calm so they can rest. Strong currents are usually a problem only with modified power filters although airstone operated box filters can create strong currents if too much air is used in their operation.

Sexing

Goldfish are not the easiest fish to tell male from female, and goldfish under one year old are just downright hard to sex.

There are some guidelines that work very well with goldfish over one year of age, but if you are trying to select a pair from a group of young goldfish, then all we can do is wish you good luck. Your best method of getting a pair of goldfish under one year of age is to buy several. Pick some of the larger fish, middle-sized fish, and smaller fish. In this way you will probably have at least

one male or one female in the group.

For mature goldfish over one year old, we can use the educated guess method and be fairly accurate although never 100%. The first item to look for is the first ray of the pectoral fin. In the male, this first ray is thicker and longer. In some of the very long finned breeds, the male's pectoral will be pointed, whereas on the female of the same breed it will have a more rounded appearance.

The next item to look at is body shape. The female usually will be larger and heavier (thicker) than the more slender male. This is easier to judge in a group of well-conditioned fish than in looking at a single goldfish.

Male goldfish, when in breeding condition, will show breeding tubercles (small white bumps) on the first ray of the pectoral fin and gill covers. Not all males will show these tubercles and males of the hooded breeds will have them visible only on the pectoral fins, as the head growth may cover the tubercles on the gill covers. (A side note about breeding tubercles is the fact that they

look very much like Ich, a parasitic disease. When first seeing these white bumps, do not panic if they are only on the gill cover and pectoral fin. If these bumps show up any place else, then treatment for Ich is advised.)

Next we move on to the last and most dependable method and that is to have your pair of goldfish spawn a fertile spawn of eggs. Notice the key word of the last sentence was **fertile.** It is not unusual for a female to release her eggs with no males present. So the saving of a few eggs to determine if they are fertile or not is necessary to determine if there is a pair in the tank.

Mature goldfish are really not too difficult to sex and in most cases an educated guess will prove to be accurate. As you become more knowledgeable and experienced with goldfish, you will find that your guesses, even in the hard-to-tell immature goldfish, will become more accurate than not, so practice is the key.

Selecting Spawners

If you are lucky enough to have several goldfish from which to choose your spawners, then you should be very selective in your choice.

When choosing spawners, never mate two fish that have the same defect. As an example, if you have a beautiful Oranda who is near perfect in every way except he only has one anal fin, do not breed him to a female with the same defect.

When matching a pair or group, try to pick individuals that will balance each other out. If you have a male Lionhead whose tail fin is too short, try mating him to a female Lionhead whose tail might be a bit long.

If you can, try to maximize on the good features of a breed. Headgrowth breeds should be bred only to those individuals that show good head growths, in hopes of improving the headgrowths. The same goes for fin type and all other breed characteristics.

When choosing your spawners, try to study the basic standard for that breed, and conform to it as closely as possible or consult a knowledgeable breeder of that breed. In this way the basic form of the young will slowly, over the years,

Facing page: Nice quality orange Bubble-eyes with good backs, good eye sacs, and good deportment. Photo by Burkhard Kahl.

conform to the accepted standard for that breed.

In making the above choices keep in mind to pick healthy, active and, most important, fish who exhibit a great deal of vigor. Vigor is hard to describe but it borders on aggressiveness. A fish who is constantly active, never sick, attacks his food and is always the first to see what's happening is a goldfish showing vigor.

Never, unless it is absolutely necessary, breed a fish that shows a physical defect, such as poor swim bladder function, weak and sickly state of being, deformed body, mouth or head, and any other obvious defects. Always try to breed for the best, healthiest and most physically perfect goldfish you can.

We hobbyists have an advantage over the commercial breeder in that we do not have to breed for high egg production and early de-coloring. We can breed for type, color, finnage, head growth, head shape, and dozens of different features that would bankrupt the commercial breeder.

We should pick breeders of high fertility, but we can forego the need for picking females just because they can spawn a huge number of eggs. Usually one to two thousand eggs is all a hobbyist can handle and if these eggs come from a high quality female of proven

In Germany these are examples of the commercial grade of Pearlscales available on the market. Photo by Burkhard Kahl.

fertility, so much the better.

As far as early and quick de-coloring goes, most hobbyists do not seem to mind waiting an extra month or two if the fish is of high quality.

When selecting your spawners, be choosy if you can. Select for type, health, fertility, vigor, and your breed will improve and be easier to care for with each succeeding generation.

Conditioning

Conditioning goldfish for breeding is not something that is done the week before you want to breed them. Conditioning goldfish is a year round project that needs careful management, good food, seasonal temperature changes, and lots of space.

The fish should be kept in as clean an environment as possible. A goldfish that is under constant environmental stress will either become diseased or will be unwilling to spawn, usually both. Proper water quality needs to be maintained at all times to keep the goldfish healthy. Good water quality is not hard to maintain, but it does

A very nice blunt-headed Chinese Lionhead. Photo by Burkhard Kahl.

need a certain amount of scheduled work in the form of water changes and filter maintenance to insure it remains constant.

Good quality food of the proper kind and in the proper amounts is a must for goldfish. Just before and during the spawning season a food high in protein, preferably live, should be fed to your spawners at least once a day. In the summer and autumn, food high in carbohydrates will help goldfish to be in the proper condition for a successful hibernation.

Although hibernation is not necessary, it does make the fish more willing to spawn and is believed to produce more vigorous fry. Goldfish are cool water fish and it is natural for them to live in water that has a temperature range of 32° to 80° F or higher. Try to keep the water temperature in the 60° to 70°F range for most of the year, but a natural slow temperature decrease in the autumn and winter should be strived for.

Do not crowd your spawners during the year. Give them lots of space and you will have spawners more willing to breed. They will also grow faster and be healthier when given extra room and uncrowded tank conditions.

The preceding was a brief explanation of year 'round conditioning for goldfish. But because we are on the subject of the breeding cycle, let us digress to the subject of food. As it was mentioned earlier, goldfish should be fed a food higher in protein at this time of year.

Earthworms, fresh or frozen, chopped or whole, are an excellent conditioning food. It is high in protein and has a mild laxative effect which is very helpful to a female full of eggs. Make sure your worms are free of pesticides and are from an area free of soil contamination. Raise your own—it is much safer.

Other good conditioning foods, either fresh or frozen, are bloodworms, Daphnia, Mosquito larvae, scrambled eggs, and some high protein prepared foods, although live foods are preferred.

Tank Set Up

A spawning tank can be a pretty Spartan affair consisting of a tank, water, filter and spawning medium. That is really all there is to it, but since this section deserves a little more than one sentence we will review each of these items, even though most of what we say has been said already.

The spawning tank should be of the long and low type with lots of surface area. For the average goldfish pair, a 30 gallon tank usually offers plenty of room. As your spawners get larger, or you increase the number of fish in the spawning group, you should use larger tanks with more surface area.

Remember never to crowd your spawners or they may feel the living conditions are too crowded and decide not to spawn.

and goldfish fry. Salt is not a necessity but the talk around town is that it does keep your goldfish healthier.

If you have successfully kept goldfish in the water in your area, then that same water can be used to successfully spawn your goldfish. The addition of one teaspoon of salt to five gallons of water has proven to be beneficial to both adult

The filter in the spawning tank need only be large enough to handle the waste by-products produced by your breeders. If the spawning tank is to be used as a hatchery tank, then a well-conditioned sponge and/or quilt-batting covered box filter will usually do the

A Chinese Ryukin with an excellent fringe and very deep markings but not the shoulder hump which Japanese Ryukins are noted for. Photo by Fred Rosenzweig.

A Broadtail Moor crossed with a Chinese Moor resulted in this Broadtail Black Moor. Photo by Fred Rosenzweig.

job for the few days the spawners are in the tank. While the spawners are in the spawning/hatchery tank, they should be fed as little as possible to keep the pollution level of the water as low as possible.

If the eggs are to be removed from the spawning tank, then filtration can be of a heavier duty nature. Power filters and/or undergravel filters can be used and the breeders fed a more normal diet.

If possible the spawning medium should be confined to one area of the spawning tank. When the eggs are to be left in the spawning-hatchery tank, the need for a lot of spawning medium can be reduced, as the eggs that attach themselves to the tank sides and bottom will hatch as well as those attached to the spawning medium.

When the eggs are to be removed, then it would be beneficial to increase the spawning medium and use both the floating and bottom type directly below the floating medium. With the increase of spawning medium, more eggs will successfully attach themselves to the medium

and therefore more eggs can be removed to the hatchery tank.

When using natural plants for the spawning medium, remember to check it closely for pests such as insect larvae, fresh water shrimp, and hydra. Remember to give the plants plenty of light to prevent them from using the oxygen in the water, which can harm both the eggs and the fry.

To clean and disinfect artificial spawning medium, a good washing in plain fresh warm water and an hour's soaking in a dark blue methylene blue and water solution will render them safe to re-use over and over again.

Of the two types of spawning medium, natural and artificial plants, the artificial is the safest and is recommended for the beginner. Although artificial spawning material does demand an initial cash outlay, the fact that, if well cared for, it will last for many years probably makes it almost as cheap to use as homegrown natural plants. (See Appendices Section for easy-to-make artificial spawning mops).

pawning

Spawning goldfish should e a well-thought-out act, ot just merely the act of utting two fish together to ee what happens. A reeding program, complete vith goals of what you wish o achieve, should be in place efore any spawning occurs. A well-thought-out breeding rogram has to include onsideration about utcrossings and line-reeding.

Outcrossing usually entails he breeding together of two r more unrelated or very istantly related goldfish. They can be of the same reed or different breeds. When this type of cross is one, the first generation F1) may not, and probably vill not, look like either of he parents. With this type f cross, a plan is a must. If ou are breeding for the reed characteristics of ither parent, then the F1 eneration should be bred ack to the parent goldfish hat has the desired haracteristics. If you are rying to combine two breed haracteristics into a new ingle multiple-breed haracteristic goldfish, then ou should mate the F1

generation to each other and with luck a few of the next generation (F2) will exhibit the desired characteristics. If this does not happen, you must set up multiple matings of the F2 generation, using several males and females so that the proper genetic matches will be made and passed on the F3 generation.

As you can see, outcrossing can take up to three or four years and demand many matings before your desired goal will be reached, if at all. Outcrossings are very time consuming and at times discouraging, but on the other hand they can also be very rewarding. They are usually resorted to only to improve vigor in a strain.

After the initial goal of an outcrossing has been reached, the time honored system of line breeding will purify and refine the breed you have developed. The mating of related fish that complement each other will, in time, give you a line of goldfish that will breed reasonably true to type (for goldfish). Remember, if even a small minority of the young goldfish resemble their parents, you are on the right road, as goldfish are always

This Black Moor, or Telescope eyed Goldfish, is losing some colors from the belly up. Photo by Fred Rosenzweig.

trying to revert back to that old silver carp ancestor.

Goldfish genetics are probably the most complex of any fish, and about the time you think you have it all figured out, they throw you a curve. Experience and trial and error are the only proven methods of achieving your goals when it comes to goldfish breeding. So try a method or a cross, and if it doesn't work out, do not be discouraged as your next try might just do the trick.

Another item to remember when spawning goldfish is that they are ravenous egg eaters. The hobbyist must be able to remove the spawn of eggs or spawners as soon as possible after the spawners lose interest in spawning. If this is not possible, then load the spawning tank with lots of spawning medium (natural and/or artificial) and hope that your goldfish will leave you enough eggs to raise.

When using more than two goldfish in a spawning group, watch out for the goldfish who is not actively participating in the spawning drive. Chances are this fish will spend its time eating the spawn, as the others are involved in the act of spawning.

Keeping the Sexes Separate. This method of spawning allows the hobbyist to determine the approximate time his goldfish will spawn. This is the biggest advantage of this system, and is useful in allowing the hobbyist the chance to watch the spawn and save the eggs.

Two large roomy tanks are necessary to hold the spawners in an uncrowded environment. The male tank and female tank can be placed side by side or in different rooms. It makes little difference to the goldfish.

If you want to have your goldfish spawn on a weekend, then your best bet is to place the spawners together on Thursday night, thus allowing them to settle down and adjust to the new tank for a day. Depending on your goldfishes' condition and readiness to spawn, you should have a spawning on Saturday or Sunday morning.

If your goldfish have not spawned as planned, try a partial water change in the evening and, with luck, the next morning might bring success. The spawners should be given at least three days to spawn or they can be eft together for as long as 10 days. If they have not

pawned in 10 days then you might consider separating them and reconditioning oth sexes for another couple f weeks before trying again. emember to feed plenty of igh protein foods and do ot overcrowd your pawners.

Permanent Spawning Set Up. Using this method, the spawners are set up in a roomy, uncrowded tank and left together during the spawning season (or longer). The hobbyist has no control over the actual spawning day and if the spawn happens while the hobbyist is away for the day, many eggs will be eaten by the spawners.

This method is used to produce lots of eggs and multiple spawns. Once the spawners start spawning, they will continue to do so every 7 to 10 days throughout the spawning season. Of course, good food and clean water are a must to maintain this schedule.

When using this method, the eggs are removed to a hatchery tank or the spawners can be moved from tank to tank as they spawn. Both methods are successful but the water quality in all of the tanks used to transfer the fish or the eggs should be very close to that of the original tank. Tanks with different water quality can shock and, in bad cases, kill the eggs or fry.

Another point to remember is that dead sperm in the spawning tanks is a very

A Chinese Lionhead. Photo by Fred Rosenzweig.

potent pollution source. Change at least 50% of the water in the spawning tank after each spawn.

Pond Spawning. For large goldfish or group spawnings (several spawners), ponds are an ideal spawning environment. As in any spawning method, control of the spawning program should be adhered to. A spawn of mixed breeds will produce only garbage, so develop a well-thought-out breeding program and stick to it.

When using a pond for spawning, it must be deep enough or large enough to prevent rapid temperature changes. Also, some means of shading should be on hand to prevent the water from becoming too green with algae. Too much algae in the form of dark green water has been said to inhibit goldfish from spawning, so control algae growth by shading.

If the fry are to be raised in the pond, it should be clean and free of hydra and insect pests. Even if the eggs are to

Top view of a Pearlscale. Note that the pearling goes over the top of the back. This is a desirable characteristic. Photo by Burkhard Kahl.

be removed to hatch elsewhere, it is a good idea that all pests be removed from the pond or they may hide in the spawning medium and be moved to the hatching location when the eggs are transferred.

Needless to say, the pond water should be clean and well aged for both the breeders' and eggs' benefit. Goldfish eggs need well oxygenated water to develop properly. A lot of decaying vegetable and fish waste can rob the water of needed oxygen, so be sure to clean the pond before the spawning starts.

The pond should have a shallow (10″–12″) area for the fish to spawn in. If this is not available, then the spawning medium should be supported so that it is in no more than 6″ to 12″ of water. Floating spawning mops or floating plants such as Water Hyacinth will serve very well as a spawning medium in deep ponds.

If the eggs are to be removed from the spawning pond, remove all plants or other items that could be used as spawning sites. If you don't you may find that clump of Water Hyacinth at the opposite end of the pond is the chosen spawning site and not your well laid-out spawning grass or mops.

Although in the U.S. most hobbyists spawn their goldfish and raise their fry in aquariums, ponds offer another avenue that should not be overlooked for the raising and keeping of goldfish. If you can, and have the resources, a pond is a good investment.

Hand Spawning. Hand spawning or the stripping of mature, properly conditioned and ready goldfish, is a very successful method of breeding goldfish. Its success all hinges on the female's being in spawning condition and willing and able to release her eggs.

So how does the hobbyist know when the female is ready? The simplest method is to catch her right after she has started to release her eggs in a normal spawn. She can then be successfully stripped of her eggs with no difficulty. It is sometimes possible to get a female to release her eggs if she is very ripe but this is seldom the case.

Males are another situation altogether. A male can be

stripped of his milt at almost anytime during the spawning season. This is one reason this method is so very useful.

Also in areas where the water may be contaminated by disease, parasites, insect pests, hydra, or pollution

A very rare and exotic Pearlscale Oranda, in red and white. The fish has two distinct head bumps and therefore is classified as a Hamanishiki. Photo by Fred Rosenzweig.

If a male proves to be uninterested in spawning, the female can be placed with another goldfish male of any goldfish breed and as soon as she starts to release her eggs the desirable male can be stripped and his milt can then be used to fertilize the female's eggs.

Another plus for stripping breeders is, if done properly, you can increase the number of fertile eggs in the spawn.

that could be harmful to eggs and fry, the breeders can be stripped by a carefully controlled method in clean water which will reduce the mortality of the spawn.

The equipment needed for hand spawning is very simple: a large bowl with 6" of clean water, a hatching tank that the bowl can fit into and a method to circulate the water, such as an airstone.

There is no single correct method to hand spawning and you will find considerable variations from breeder to breeder. If you are using a method that works, or if you have been shown a different method than that which we will describe, by all means use it as you will probably be just as successful.

Hand spawning is done simply by netting the ripe female first and testing her by cradling her in the palm of one hand while with the thumb of the other hand gently stroking the abdomen from the dorsal area to the anal region. She should, if she is ready, release her eggs with very little pressure and in fact she may release some eggs while being netted. If the female is ready, replace her in the tank and quickly catch the desired male(s). The male's milt (sperm) is stripped from him in the same method the female was tested. The male should be stripped directly into the bowl of clean water. The female is then re-netted and stripped into the same bowl, taking care to distribute the eggs evenly throughout the bowl. If the female is large you may want to use more than one bowl so as to not crowd too many eggs into one bowl. Try to spread the eggs evenly over the entire bowl. Do not clump the eggs all together or they will die.

Red and white Oranda with a lovely head. The head growth is a little below the eye and this is a fault. Photo by Fred Rosenzweig.

Next, the water containing the eggs and milt should be gently circulated for 30 minutes. This is where an airstone comes in handy, or you can stir the water with your hand or use a spoon.

After the eggs and milt have been together for 30 minutes, pour off the water and gently rinse the eggs that are now stuck to the bowl with water of the same temperature and quality. Gently rinse the eggs two or three times to remove the excess sperm. The reason for all of this careful rinsing to remove the sperm is to prevent the sperm, as they die, from polluting the hatchery tank's water. When rinsing the eggs, do not be afraid that they will be washed out of the bowl. Goldfish eggs are very adhesive and will usually stay in the bowl even with vigorous rinsing.

Place the bowl into a hatchery tank making sure it is totally submerged. Next, set up an airstone near the bowl to be sure the eggs are properly oxygenated and that no scum will form on the water's surface. This circulation does not need to be heavy, but it does need to be heavy enough to ensure a fresh flow of water over the eggs.

Now to mention a few alternate methods to show you how variable this method is. A spawning mop or spawning grass can be placed in the bowl and the eggs can be stuck to it. Using this method, the spawning medium can be removed and placed in the hatchery tank which makes getting freshly oxygenated water to the eggs much easier. Also, a shallower water level can be maintained in the hatchery tank, as there is no need to submerge the bowl.

A female can be stripped in several bowls and then each bowl can be fertilized with different males. This method allows for a very controlled breeding program when used with a proven female and can be very beneficial in weeding out poor quality males.

It really doesn't matter if the male or the female is stripped first. The advantage to stripping the female last is that an egg will absorb its weight in water very soon after it is ejected from the female, and this helps the sperm come in contact and penetrate the egg easier.

Hand spawning should only be attempted by the beginning goldfish breeder after having several successful natural spawns. It is very important that the female be in the proper spawning condition. This can be recognized only through experience with observing the natural spawning cycle, so go slowly and take your time to study the spawning goldfish.

Temperature

Goldfish usually spawn in water temperatures in the high 60° F range to the low 70° F range. Goldfish can and do spawn in temperatures outside of this range, but for proper development of the eggs and fry of the very fancy goldfish breeds, the temperature should stay within the 66° to 74° F range.

Now that you know the proper spawning temperatures, a few words about how temperature can be used in conditioning and motivating reluctant breeders into spawning, and also a few hints and rumors worth passing on.

Although conditioning

A top American strain of Ranchu. This has a nice color pattern and a very round, oval body. Photo by Fred Rosenzweig.

65

goldfish for breeding is a year 'round process, female goldfish fill out very quickly with eggs if the water temperature is in the 60° to 65° F range. This temperature range is usually cool enough to prevent spawning, but to make sure, remove all spawning medium that might prompt the goldfish to spawn.

Goldfish start to spawn very early in the morning and usually are through by noon. Sometimes reluctant to spawn goldfish can be prompted to spawn by allowing the temperature of the spawning tank to cool down overnight a few degrees and then raise the temperature a few degrees first thing in the morning. This is easily done by using an aquarium heater attached to a timer that has been set to come on in the very early morning and off at noon. This method may have to be used for several weeks or it may work the next day. Such is the unpredictability of some of our golden friends.

When using a thermometer, it is very important that it be tested to assure it is accurate. If you have several thermometers, place them all in the same aquarium. If you are like most of us and use the standard cheap aquarium thermometers, you will probably notice that none of

A high-cheeked Chinese Lionhead. Photo by Fred Rosenzweig.

these thermometers will have the exact same reading. So if you plan to breed goldfish, it is a wise hobbyist who will buy a very accurate thermometer. A good source of accurate thermometers is a store specializing in candy-making equipment. You will find that they have dial type, bi-metal thermometers that have a range from 0° to 400° F. These are nice as they can be tested by placing them in boiling water and matching their reading to the temperature that water boils in your elevation (212° F at sea level). Many of these candy thermometers can be adjusted and this type is worth the few extra dollars it costs to buy them.

It has been claimed that when eggs develop at 68° F, fin development is at its best. This claim was made in reference to short, doubletailed breeds such as Lionheads, Ranchus, etc. It has also been claimed that 72° F is the best temperature to incubate the eggs of the long finned breeds such as Orandas, Ryukins, etc. Using these two claims as a basis and knowing the poor accuracy of most cheap thermometers, it is recommended that a temperature of 70° F is safe for incubating goldfish eggs. A great deal of testing needs to be done in the area of egg incubation temperatures and, as of yet, there are no conclusive results. So if you are in the position to do some testing and experimenting, you should try to determine which temperature is best for you and your goldfish breed.

Another claim has been made in reference to the vigor of the fry and the temperature at which the eggs were incubated. Once again 68° F was the considered optimum temperature for hatching vigorous fry. In fact, many hobbyists have gone to a lot of effort to make sure that their eggs develop at this temperature. Air conditioned hatchery rooms and hatchery tanks with a heater kept inside another tank filled with ice water are all methods that have been used in warm climates to keep the water temperature at 68° F.

Needless to say, a lot of testing has been done and is being done with temperature and goldfish eggs, fry, and adults. More testing in all of

An orange and white Oranda with a white head growth. Photo by Fred Rosenzweig.

these areas needs to be done and the results need to be carefully recorded and passed on to other hobbyists so that they may be duplicated and confirmed. Only in this way will we be able to determine the optimum temperatures in relation to goldfish culture.

So what's stopping you? Let's get to work.

Caring for the Eggs

Goldfish eggs were heaven-sent for those of us too busy, lazy, or apathetic. The reason for this is simple. Once the eggs have been laid, the hobbyist need only make sure the water stays clean, well oxygenated, and the temperature remains in the safe zone, and that's all there is to it.

The eggs of goldfish are very adhesive. Once they become attached to the spawning medium, they usually hang on to it like teenagers to their first love. This adhesion makes it possible to easily rinse the eggs and spawning medium as well as to transport the eggs without fear of losing them.

If the hatchery tank's water is clean and free of decaying organic material, it is not necessary to treat the water with fungicides (Methylene Blue). Even though it will take anywhere from 3 to 8 days for the eggs to hatch (depending on the temperature), it is only a very rare or extremely heavy fungus infection that will attack fertile goldfish eggs. For this same reason, it is not necessary to remove the infertile fungus-infected goldfish eggs from a spawn as they do very little harm to the spawn in general.

Goldfish eggs need a very well oxygenated water. This is easily accomplished by placing the eggs in a very roomy hatchery tank or pond. Another method is to use an airstone to circulate the water. This has the added benefit of breaking up any surface scum that forms on the water's surface. The airstone should be allowed to run just hard enough to create a gentle current as this will be enough to move freshly oxygenated water over and around the eggs.

As mentioned in the section on temperature, the eggs should not be exposed to extreme temperature changes. The more constant the temperature, the more predictable the hatching time can be calculated. At 68° F goldfish eggs will hatch in 4 days. You should be able to see the fry's eyes in two days and the infertile eggs will turn milky in less than 24 hours. Fertile eggs will

Facing page: An orange and white Ranchu. Photo by Fred Rosenzweig.

remain clear and you will be able to watch the fry develop until they hatch.

Novice goldfish breeders usually panic the first time they spawn goldfish for, on the second day when examining the spawn, it will usually look like the whole spawn is infertile. The cloudy opaque infertile eggs are so easily seen it is simple to overlook the fertile clear eggs. The best advice at this time is to have patience and wait for several days to allow the good eggs to hatch. That hopeless spawn will probably end up giving you more fry than you will know what to do with. So be patient and relax. You will need the rest as you will become very busy shortly feeding, caring for and culling baby goldfish.

The ideal water depth for hatching eggs and raising fry under 10 days of age is 6"— less than this is subject to rapid temperature changes. Although water depths of more than 6" are all right to use, 10" should be considered the maximum water depth for hatching goldfish eggs and raising fry under 10 days old. Just be sure the water is not too deep or the current too strong to prevent the fry from reaching the surface for their first gulp of air by the third day after they hatch.

Care of Fry to 10 Days of Age

Goldfish eggs hatch in approximately 4 days at 68° F. If your eggs do not hatch when they are exactly four days old, do not panic, as this time will vary somewhat from spawn to spawn, as well as goldfish breed to goldfish breed.

When the eggs hatch, they are pretty helpless, as they are not much more than 2 eyes attached to the egg yolk with a tail. For the first few days (usually two or three days at 68° F) the fry need no food as they get all of their nourishment from their attached egg yolk. The only thing the hobbyist needs to do is maintain an even temperature in the 68° to 72° F range and to furnish a means of gently circulating the water.

When the fry are about three days old you will notice that they will dart to the water's surface. Many hobbyists believe that the fry are trying to gulp a bubble of air in order to fill their air

bladders. Adult goldfish will dart to the surface and gulp air and many believe they do this to adjust the pressure in their air bladders. Whatever the reasons for this behavior, the hobbyist should try to keep any surface scum from forming on the hatchery tank. If this scum is not

removed or broken up by aeration, you may be unlucky enough to have a tank full of belly sliders, or fry that may have difficulty in swimming properly.

As the fry absorb the egg yolk, they move very little and will hang from the spawning medium, on the tank's side, filter, heater, or will lay motionless on the bottom of the tank. Try to disturb the fry as little as possible at this time, which should be easy as there is very little that the fry needs from the hobbyist at this point.

When the fry are between two and three days of age, they will start to swim horizontally and will start to search for food. At this stage of their development, some hobbyists will raise the temperature of the hatchery tank by 2-4 degrees. This helps increase the appetite of the fry and will increase their growth.

When the fry become free swimming (swimming horizontally), the hobbyist must furnish enough food of the proper size to insure the fry do not go hungry. Live food is preferred, such as baby Daphnia, baby Brine Shrimp, Microworms, Rotifers, etc. Dry foods or prepared foods are a poor second choice with the exception of a boiled egg yolk that has been liquefied. Egg yolk must be fed with care as it can foul the hatchery tank's water very quickly, so use it in moderation.

In all fairness, some goldfish fry in a spawn can be raised to adult goldfish on prepared or dry food and nothing else. Commercial liquid fry foods are a fair first food for fry. Dry food, ground to the fineness of flour and sprinkled on the water's surface or mixed with water, is also a fair first food for goldfish.

When feeding goldfish fry, you must take care to notice if the fry are eating what you are feeding. A flashlight is a handy tool at this time. By shining the flashlight on the fry, the food will show up very clearly as a thin line running almost the length of the fry's body. Also, another point that needs to be made is never abruptly change the food that the fry are eating to another type of food. Do all food changes slowly to give

You can tell a strain is clean when you see matched fish like these 6-month-old calico Veiltails. Photo by Fred Rosenzweig.

them a chance to locate and adjust to the new food.

Cleanliness is a must when raising goldfish. Successful goldfish breeders try to clean and change part of the water in each fry tank daily. To remove the bottom sediment, a small piece of airline tubing with a rigid plastic tube about 12–16 inches long in one end. will allow the hobbyist to remove the waste without removing too many fry. To do a 10% water change or more, you can use a larger diameter syphon hose with a sponge or filter floss wrapped over the end. This will enable the water to be quickly syphoned without the bother of sucking up a large number of fry.

When you syphon a fry tank, it is almost impossible not to syphon up fry in the process. To save time, you should syphon the water into a large white plastic bowl. By positioning the discharge end of the syphon so that the water will circulate around the bowl in a whirlpool fashion, all of the waste will be collected in the very center of the bowl. This makes the fry easier to catch and return to the hatchery tank.

A net should not be used to catch fry under 10 days of age. Either use a small cup to catch the fry with some water or use a large kitchen baster to suck the fry up. The kitchen baster is a very useful tool in raising goldfish fry. It can be used to remove small amounts of waste from the fry tank. It is useful in culling young fry, for collecting baby Brine Shrimp and dozens of other tasks are made quicker and easier.

As mentioned earlier in the filtration section, the fry tank at this time needs a constant, gentle, biological filtration system in the form of a well conditioned sponge filter or a quilt-batting wrapped box filter. This biological filtration is important more for its water purification than for waste removal, as ammonia and nitrites are certain death to the goldfish fry under 10 days of age.

If you are raising fry from one of the fancier breeds, then when the fry are 10 feeding days old (13–14 days since hatching), you should start culling all the fry who do not have the desired early characteristics of the breed.

74

This is an attractive calico Oranda goldfish. According to current judging, the white area should be bluer, but the contrast makes the fish very attractive. Photo by Burkhard Kahl.

Care of Fry 10 to 30 Days of Age

After the first culling at 10 days of age, it is time to separate your goldfish fry into size groups and put each group into their own tanks. For approximate fry-to-tank densities refer to Section on Tank Size. Crowding of the fry at this time can lead to the loss of the entire spawn if a disease or a parasitic problem gets a foothold.

If possible, daily cleaning and water changes (10%–20%) are still a necessity that will ensure healthy fry. Remember that the fresh replacement water used in water changes should be the same temperature as the fry tank and should be free of compressed gases and chlorine or chloramine. A group of 5 gallon plastic buckets are very handy items to age replacement water as well as for dozens of other chores around your aquariums.

Even though your fry have more than doubled in size, their food size requirements

Top view of a Chinese Lionhead. Note the bluntness of the head and straightness of the back. This is a prime example of a champion German-bred Lionhead. Photo by Burkhard Kahl.

will remain pretty much the same. Screened Daphnia, baby Brine Shrimp, Microworms, powdered dry food and if the fry are large enough, a small amount of paste food can be given at this time. Syphon out all uneaten food every night to prevent polluting the fry's water. If you can, try to feed a variety of food so the fry will become accustomed to eating different ones. This is important to prevent them from going hungry in case something were to happen to your basic food source. A good feeding schedule would be a live food in the morning, a powdered food at noon and another live food in the evening.

If you are unable to feed at noon, then a paste food fed in the morning along with the live food will last all day and will give the more adventuresome fry something to eat all day. As soon as some fry learn to eat paste food, it won't be long before the rest of the fry will copy what their big brothers are doing and will eat it also.

Goldfish fry should be fed as often as possible and small amounts given 10 times a day is not too often, but for most of us, feeding that often is impossible. Goldfish fry can be raised successfully on as little as two feedings per day. Of course with fewer

your feeding schedule, you should stay as consistent as you can.

As your fry approach 30 feeding days of age, the filtration of their tank should be increased by adding another well-conditioned sponge filter or quilt-batting wrapped box filter. Fry at this stage can also be moved to a tank with a well-

This is a lovely 6-year-old Chinese Lionhead with beautiful, delicate markings and a relatively straight back. Photo by Fred Rosenzweig.

feedings, growth will be slower but over the long run these slow but steady growers can be just as nice as the fast growers. The important point to remember is once you have established

conditioned undergravel filter. The biggest problem with using undergravel filters is that a lot of food will be lost in the gravel which prevents the fry from grazing on the bottom of the tank.

This means you must feed small amounts more often or use a live food, such as screened Daphnia, that will swim in the water until eaten.

At 30 feeding days of age, if you have not done so already, cull the fry to remove defective non-standard fish. If culling has not reduced the number of fry to the proper fry-to-tank density, then spread the fry into more tanks to reduce the danger of overcrowding. Culling should be an on-going process. An easy way to cull is to use your syphon hose to remove defective fish. This can be done daily as you syphon off the waste in each fry tank. Daily culling helps reduce the overall time and work needed in culling an entire spawn of goldfish fry, and using the syphon for culling does not increase your daily cleaning time by very much.

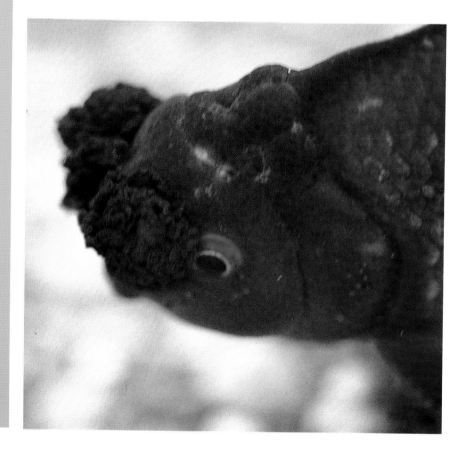

A closeup of the head region of a brown Pompon Oranda. This is a rare color and rare combination. Photo by Fred Rosenzweig.

Care of Fry 30 to 60 Days of Age

By the time your goldfish fry reach 30 days of age, they will start to look more like small goldfish rather than two eyes and a small tailfin (or fins) attached by a slender stick. You should be able to tell which scale group they belong to (metallic, nacreous or matt). The fins should be easily seen so they can be judged for size, shape, completeness, and symmetry.

You will also notice one other thing about your goldfish spawn. You will have fry as large as one inch long and as small as ¼ inch long. Goldfish grow at different rates and it is very important that they be divided into size groups. Each group should have its own tank or the larger group will use the smaller group for food. Usually dividing this spawn into two or more groups will prevent any problems with the larger fry picking on the smaller fry.

As the fry grow larger, Microworms, baby Brine Shrimp and sifted Daphnia are starting to get pretty small to satisfy the appetites of your goldfish fry. If you haven't already done so, now is a good time to introduce dry foods and/or paste food to the daily diet of the fry. Of course larger Daphnia, small Bloodworms, small Mosquito larvae and other smaller sized live foods are the preferred choices to feed at this time, but many, if not most of us goldfish hobbyists, will not have access to these live foods. It is very important that the fry not go hungry, so feed the best food you can as this will ensure the steady growth of your goldfish fry.

By the time the fry are 30 days old, they can be kept in water deeper than the six inches in which they spent their first couple of weeks. A water depth of 10 to 12 inches is a safe level to maintain from this time on. Raise the water level slowly over a period of several days to prevent the fry from being shocked due to a rapid change in water quality and depth.

With the increased water volume in the tank, the need for daily water changes is lessened somewhat. All uneaten food should still be removed every night, but a 10-20% water change every

A beautiful full-bodied Pearlscale which is, unfortunately, missing some of its scales. The body pearling does not extend across its back, but its finnage and body are excellent. Photo by Bob Mertlich.

two to three days is enough to prevent water quality problems. Of course this is assuming that the fry are eating most of the food that they are being fed and that the tank is not overcrowded and has a good filtration system in operation.

Usually in an uncrowded fry tank your two sponge or two quilt-batting wrapped box filters will handle the waste produced by fry in a 20 to 35 gallon tank. But being the type of people we goldfish hobbyists are, we will tend to overcrowd our fry tanks by not culling when we should or by trying to keep too many marginal fish. If this is the case, you must increase filtration by adding more filters or by adding an undergravel filter or power filter to your tank.

When using a power filter, try to use a power intake model. By placing a coarse sponge over the end of the

intake, you will be able to keep the fry from being sucked into the filter and killed. A good portable undergravel filter can be made by using a goldfish bowl undergravel filter plate in a shallow plastic bowl filled with one or two inches of gravel. The gravel should be fine enough to prevent trapping the smaller fry and yet large enough to ensure a rapid water flow. No matter what type of filtration system or systems you use, try to control or reduce the currents created by the filters, as the fry are still too small and weak to fight strong currents.

From here on out the easiest way to cull is daily, with the food container in one hand and the culling net in the other hand. A rule to remember in preventing damage to the fry—*"only net fish to be culled."* When moving the better fry, use a bowl or a cup and transfer the fry with some of the water in their tank. At any stage of growth or age, a goldfish is easily damaged by using a net, especially the fins and scales. If you can, use your wet hands or some other means to move your

soon-to-be-high-quality goldfish.

Care of Fry 60 Days and Older

Goldfish fry two months old and older will start to take on some of the breed characteristics of their parents if they are pure breeds.

The metallic scaled fry will start to de-color, which means they will start to turn pale orange from the olive green color that they were. Some breeds will turn sooner than others and some fry in the spawn may never change or may take years to change to orange. Breeds which change to orange will go through a darkening phase, which in some fry will approach black. This darkening phase is usually short-lived and the orange color will appear, starting on the abdomen, and will quickly move upward to the dorsal area, replacing all of the dark or black pigment. Breeds with colors other than orange (or red and red and white), such as blue, brown, and black will start to gradually change to these colors.

When the fry have decolored, they will usually be a pale orange which over time will darken. To improve the color of all goldfish, they nacreous scale group will start to develop their color in their second month. The colors to show up first are

A top view of a Black Moor. Note how the telescope-eyes bulge out. Photo by Burkhard Kahl.

should be given some natural sunlight for part of the day. Although this is not always possible for the average hobbyist, a goldfish's color is never at its best without being exposed to some sunlight.

Goldfish fry from the usually black and orange. If the fry are from a strain that has blue, this color will show up later and may take many months before it starts to show its true color and pattern. Some highly developed calico breeds will change their colors as they get older and hobbyists who breed these goldfish should make every effort to keep their spawners for at least 2 years to determine the color quality of their calicos.

Goldfish of the matt scale group are basically pink with no reflective tissue (guanine) in their scales, gill covers or eyes. If color is the goal of the hobbyist, matts offer very little in color although a very small percentage may show some color. If breed characteristics other than color are being bred for (finnage, head growth, etc.), matts can give a very attractive contrast to their more colorful brothers and sisters. Matts can be picked out when the fry are very young by looking for their solid black eyes and pink bodies.

The food you feed your young goldfish should be higher in protein than you would normally feed to your older goldfish. Make sure that your short bodied breeds get enough carbohydrates so that they will develop the full bodies that these breeds are known for.

If possible, try to feed some live food daily. Frozen food such as Brine Shrimp, Bloodworms, Daphnia, etc., are a good second choice if live foods are not available.

There are some good dry foods on the market which make a fair third choice to feed your spawn of goldfish. Make sure the food is small enough for the fry to eat and be careful not to overfeed as water pollution is a constant battle the hobbyist must deal with.

Homemade paste foods with cooked grains or gelatin as the binding base are a good food for older goldfish fry. A clump can be added in the morning and the fry can nibble at it all day long, which gives them a constant dependable supply of food. Remember to remove every night any food excess that has not been eaten.

The fry at two months are usually large enough to live in a tank with any type of filtration that is acceptable for adult goldfish. Remember, goldfish are not happy in heavy currents, so when using high current producing filters, every effort should be made to deflect and reduce these currents.

As mentioned in earlier

sections, culling should be done often to allow the better high quality fry more food and room to grow to their potential. A special culling net, kept within reach of the fry tank, will ensure that culling is done promptly when a defective fish is first noticed. If you end up having to search for your net, then chances are the job will be postponed until it reaches a point where it will have to be done in a crisis situation to prevent gross overcrowding of the fry's tank.

Culling

Of all the necessary jobs we take on when raising a spawn of goldfish, culling is probably the easiest to postpone, and yet it is one of the most important chores that has to be done *often* in order to raise quality goldfish fry.

In the preceding section, we mentioned when to cull and some easy methods to cull. In this section we will deal with the subjects of what to look for when culling your goldfish fry and some step-by-step methods in culling. Also in this section

we will deal mostly with the doubletailed breeds as they entail much more culling than the singletailed breeds.

When culling goldfish fry at 10 days of age, it is best to move the fry to a shallow white bowl for easier examination. Remember not to use a net. Transfer the fry with a cup or a square plastic container and some of the aquarium water that they are in.

Ten day old fry are not much more than two eyes, a spinal column and a tail fin, so these are the items we cull for. Goldfish have two eyes—make sure you cull for this feature. The spinal column should be straight and should have no bends in it. These first two items should be responsible for the removal of only a few fry. The culling of the singletailed fry from the doubletailed breeds will probably remove more fry at 10 days of age than any other single defect.

By looking down on them, it is very easy to tell the singletailed fry from the doubletailed. When culling goldfish fry, you cannot go wrong if you keep this little thought in mind: *"when in*

This is a very rare mixed-breed black and red Telescope-eyed Oranda Fringetail with a magnificent balance of color. Photo by Fred Rosenzweig.

oubt, cull." If you have to scratch your head and think about culling a very young fry, chances are the fry is mediocre at best and is not worth the space or time to raise it. You must examine fry at every culling for the double tail, as at times one of the tails will stop developing or will become deformed in some way.

Other items to look for in the first few major cullings are runts, poor swimmers and belly sliders. These are faults that will not correct themselves as the fry get older so cull them early to save space and food.

When the fry are over 30 days of age, a special culling tank or a goldfish bowl comes in handy. At this age, the fry should be culled by viewing from above and from the side. When viewing from above, look for runts, single tails, and bent backs. Viewing from the side will allow you to cull for humped backs, poor swimmers, belly sliders, missing fins, or fins where they are not supposed to be.

When examining the finnage of a goldfish fry, pay special attention to symmetry, position and, above all, make sure it's all there. The tail of a double tailed goldfish has four lobes with two lobes on each side. The two tail fins should be separated from each other right down to the caudal peduncle (base of the tail). It is a rare fish who has this complete separation but it is a standard to reach for.

A doubletailed goldfish whose tail is completely joined at the top is called a web tail. Another common form of misshapen tail is a tripod tail. A tripod tailed goldfish has one lobe on top with two lobes dividing off from the middle of the single lobe (looks like an upside-down "Y"). When viewing the double tail fins from the rear, the angle of the tail should form an inverted (upside-down) "V" in most breeds. There are breeds (Tosas, Jikins, etc.) that have a specific type of tail that the breed is known for, so study their standards carefully. Also goldfish from different parts of the world will have different angles to the inverted "V" shape (Butterfly Tail, Chinese Lionheads), so it is helpful to understand the breed standards of your goldfish fry.

As your fry get older, you will notice that some of the tail fins will develop bends and grow at unnatural angles. Some of this has been caused by careless handling by the hobbyist but mostly it is due to genetic defects and these fry should be culled unless they have other exceptional breed characteristics which must be used in future breeding programs. Every effort should be made to breed only those fish who have finnage as close to the breed standard as possible.

In a doubletailed breed the anal fins should be paired. They should be of the same size and shape and carried between the tail fins. If you find you have an exceptional fish except that it has only one anal fin, this fish can be used for breeding, but only if its mate has both anal fins. Never breed to each other two goldfish with the same defect as this only ingrains the defect into the breed line.

For those breeds which have dorsal fins, make sure it is all there and in the right place. As strange as that last sentence sounds, it is very common to find fry with

incomplete dorsals and with dorsals too far back or too far forward of where they are supposed to be. All dorsaled breeds should have dorsal fins that are held high and erect with no major bends in the dorsal. Goldfish with short dorsals or dorsals that curl to one side should not be used in your breeding program.

In culling the dorsalless breeds you will more than likely lose more fish to defects in the dorsal area than to any other single defect. Defects from minor bumps, to dorsal ray spikes, to complete dorsals can be expected. In well-finned, linebred, dorsalless goldfish you can expect to lose 30% or more of the fry due to dorsal area defects. In most cases, you can expect more than this as most breeds are not very well fixed due to outcrossings. If a fry exhibits bumps, spikes or poor curvature along the dorsal area, usually it only gets

This is a young, ordinary petshop quality Chinese Lionhead. Photo by Michael Gilroy.

87

worse as it gets older. Therefore, cull these fry early.

To cull for basic body shape, the fry should be at least three months old. As just about every breed of goldfish has its own distinctive body curvature and shape, you should study the breed standard as well as communicate with other knowledgeable hobbyists to determine the correct body shape for your goldfish. In general, the body should curve from head to tail in a smooth unbroken line. No bumps or major angle changes (possible exception is the Japanese Ranchu) should be noticeable. The body should be formed in such a way that the fins are held erect which will allow the goldfish to swim smoothly. An example of a poorly formed fish is an Oranda with long tail fins and a very short tail portion of the body (rear edge of the dorsal to the base of the tail fin). This type of body does not allow the goldfish the strength to handle the long tail and will force him to

This lovely red and black Oranda is gradually losing its black pigmentation and eventually will probably be solid red. Photo by Fred Rosenzweig.

This 6-month old Ranchu is the best bred in America. It is shown in its all-white form, but eventually the fins will probably pick up some red markings. Photo by Fred Rosenzweig.

obble and swim in a jerky motion.

When culling a spawn of oldfish, always try to select r vigor, strength, and good rowth rates. Select fish hich are not fussy eaters nd which grow well on the ood you have available to eed them. Choose goldfish hich do well in your water nd which do not suffer near eath if you are a few days ate in cleaning their tank. ook for the aggressive eater nd avoid the shy and meek. eep these items in mind when selecting for color, finnage and body shape and you will develop a line of goldfish that will be as carefree as goldfish can be.

Remember: *"when in doubt, cull, and cull, and cull."* It is impossible for the average hobbyist to raise all of the fry from just one spawn of goldfish. By reducing the number of fry very early, you will save time, food, money, tank space, and will end up with higher quality goldfish.

Fry Foods

Infusoria: These very small plants and animals (many are single-celled) are not much used by the goldfish hobbyists who raise their fry in aquariums. Hobbyists who have ponds find that infusoria will grow naturally and at least at first will help to supplement the diet of their goldfish fry. The reason this food is not used more often by hobbyists is that goldfish fry are almost too large to feed on it and there are larger foods that are easier and more dependable for the purpose.

To culture infusoria is simple. Place several grains of wheat, corn, peas or crushed lettuce leaves in a quart of aquarium water. Allow this to age for several days until it becomes cloudy. After the water becomes cloudy, expose the culture to bright sunlight for several days to encourage a growth of algae and single-celled animals to grow. To ensure a constant supply, several one gallon or larger containers must be started at one day intervals. A microscope or a powerful magnifying glass is a handy tool for determining the density of the infusoria culture. It takes a great deal of infusoria to feed a spawn of goldfish so be ready to introduce other fry foods as early as possible.

Crustacea: These are without a doubt one of the best foods to feed goldfish fry if you have a clean, pest-free, dependable source. If the hobbyist is lucky enough to have such a source, then enough can be fed at one time to last several hours which will reduce the need to feed many times during the day. Don't feed too many as they will compete with the fry for oxygen.

Small crustaceans can be gathered from small ponds to large lakes and, as long as these are free from harmful pollution and insecticides, they make a great food. To gather them, you will need a very fine net such as large brine shrimp nets sold at most larger pet shops. Transport your catch back home in a container full of water with adequate surface area to prevent their suffocation and death.

Moena and Cyclops can be fed to the smallest of goldfish fry with little or no sorting for size. Daphnia need to be screened into different sizes

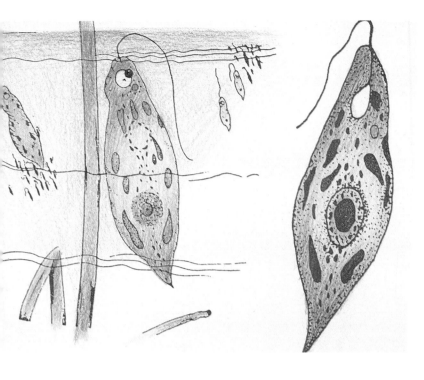

s only baby Daphnia can be
ed to very young goldfish
ry. To screen Daphnia,
atch a net full of Daphnia in
 fine but porous net. Place
he net over a bowl and then
our water into the net of
)aphnia. This should wash
he smaller Daphnia through
he net and into the bowl.
Remember to feed only
nough to last several hours
r you may deplete the
xygen in the aquarium's
vater to the point that it will
ill the fry.
Brine shrimp Nauplii: By
atching Brine Shrimp eggs
n salt water you can furnish

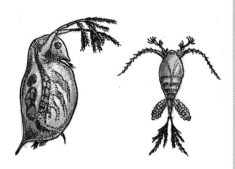

Larger food for growing goldfish fry are *Daphnia*, to the left, and *Cyclops*, to the right. Petshops often sell live *Daphnia*.

your goldfish fry with a pest-
free, nourishing food with
only a moderate amount of
hassle and expense. There
are two basic methods to
hatch Brine Shrimp eggs and
both methods give good
results and have their
advocates.

91

Enlarged between 10 and 20 times, these are adult brine shrimp, the species which grows in the San Francisco area. Photo courtesy of San Francisco Bay Brand, Inc.

The Tray Method is probably the simplest and quickest method to harvest. All you will need is a tray that will safely hold salt water without corroding, a divider of some sort to divide the tray in half, and a lightproof lid to cover the egg side of the tray. To set the tray up, simply fill it with hatching solution and place the divider in such a way that it divides the tray in half but does not go all the way to the bottom of the tray. Place the Brine Shrimp eggs in one half of the tray and cover with the lightproof cover. This will put the eggs in a dark area to hatch. As the eggs hatch the Brine Shrimp nauplii are attracted to the bright half of the tray where they can be syphoned up with a kitchen baster and collected in a brine shrimp net. Allow the excess salt water to drain from the net before feeding the shrimp to your fry.

The other method uses heavy aeration to circulate the eggs in the hatching solution. This method is easier to set up than the tray method but it takes a little longer to harvest the shrimp after they hatch.

The container for this method should be tall, narrow and, if possible, smaller at the bottom than the top. This is not as hard as it sounds, as with a little wood work, a stand can be made to hold one gallon plastic milk cartons, two liter soft drink containers, and other plastic containers upside down. Cut the bottom off these containers, fill them with hatching solution, place an airstone in the bottom, sprinkle the Brine Shrimp eggs over the top, and turn on enough air to keep the eggs from settling to the bottom. To harvest, shut the air off and allow the egg shells to settle (usually 5 to 10 minutes). Then remove the shrimp with a syphon or kitchen baster into a brine shrimp net. Allow the excess salt water to drain from the net before feeding to the fry.

Brine Shrimp eggs hatch best when the temperature is in the 70° to 85°F range. The warmer the hatching solution, the quicker the eggs hatch. If you want to use the hatching solution again, strain out all of the egg shells and unhatched eggs from the solution before

re-using it. Many hobbyists believe that re-using the hatching brine allows harmful bacteria and fungus to build up in it, which can cause the fry to become sick. To be safe, at least at first, use new hatching solution and wash the container after each hatch to avoid disease in the fry tank.

Brine shrimp do not hatch well in the dark. Hatch them in a brightly lighted area or build a Brine Shrimp hatchery with its own light source. The light in the hatchery will not only produce the correct light conditions for a better hatch but will provide some heat to keep the hatchery warm.

A good hatching brine solution is:

1 gallon water (treat for chlorine, chloramine, ammonia if needed)
4 tablespoons salt (6-8 tablespoons if using coarse Rock Salt)
1–2 tablespoons Epsom salt (optional)
1 teaspoon to 1 tablespoon baking soda (pH 7.5 to 8.0) (optional)

The specific gravity should be between 1020 and 1025. If you plan on hatching a lot of Brine Shrimp eggs, please invest in a hydrometer and a pH test kit to insure constant good hatches. At 80°F most brands of Brine Shrimp eggs should hatch in less than 36 hours.

Microworms: These tiny worms are a good food for very small goldfish fry. They are propagated in a cereal base: cooked oatmeal, cornmeal, wheat heart cereal, wheat germ, High Protein Baby Cereal or a combination of some of them. The trick in preparing the base is to make it moist enough for the Microworm to thrive, and yet it has to be thick enough to keep the worms from turning it into a soup after several days of growing in it.

The best base for just keeping Microworms for a considerable length of time is lightly cooked cornmeal. Unfortunately, it does not produce many worms to feed to your fry. Probably the best culture medium for high worm production is High Protein Baby Cereal. Unfortunately it does not last very long before going sour.

A good culture for high production and a fair culture life consists of ½ High Protein Baby Cereal and ½

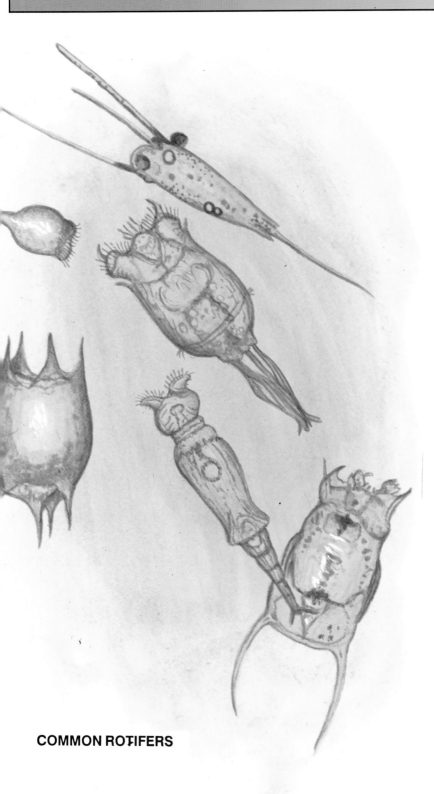

If you have a small microscope, murky water might reveal small animals such as protozoans and rotifers. Rotifers are the natural food for many small fish fry.

COMMON ROTIFERS

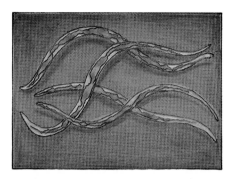

PREPARING MICROWORMS

These tiny worms are excellent food for the fry. A lightly cooked cornmeal base or, alternatively, a high protein baby cereal is inoculated with worm culture. A small dish with a cover is used. As the worms climb up the side of the container they can be removed and fed to your goldfish fry.

Cream-of-Wheat Cereal. Mix this with enough water to make a thick soupy mixture. Cook or microwave long enough to help the cereals absorb the excess water. Place about one inch of this culture medium in the bottom of a bowl that has a tight fitting lid (cut four or five small holes in the lid). Sprinkle the top of the cereal culture medium with enough yeast to lightly cover the entire surface. The yeast acts as a food for the worm and keeps mold off the culture medium until the worms have established themselves.

It will take about four or five days at room temperature (70° F) for the worms to become established. At this point, stir the content of the culture very well, add a sprinkle of yeast and presto—in a few hours you will have thousands of worms climbing the sides of the container. Remove these worms from the container's sides with your finger or a wet cotton swab. Stir the contents of each Microworm container every four to five days, adding a sprinkle of yeast and you will have a high producing culture for at least three weeks. Since it takes four to five days to start a culture, it is a good idea to start new cultures once a week to insure a constant supply of Microworms.

Liquefied Boiled Egg Yolk: When fed with great care, liquefied boiled egg yolk is a great first food for goldfish fry if no live food small enough is available. Care has to be exercised in how much is fed and the prompt removal of all excess egg yolk is important to prevent rapid water pollution which can kill the entire spawn.

To prepare this helpful early fry food is easy. Boil an egg for 10 minutes. Remove the egg yolk and place it in a blender with just enough water to allow the blender to liquefy the egg yolk. A small medicine bottle with a dropper can be bought from any pharmacy and makes a great container to hold the liquefied egg yolk. Refrigerated, the egg yolk solution will keep for five to six days, at which time a new solution should be made.

Since the size of the aquarium and the number of fry in it will determine how much you will need to feed,

no exact amount can be given. As a guide, figure one drop to every one to two gallons of water and go from there. Your fry can be fed liquefied egg yolk until they are seven days old at which time they will need a larger size food.

Powdered Dry Food: Although it is possible to raise goldfish fry on nothing but various sizes of powdered food, this really should be used as a supplemental food and not the only food.

Finely powdered dry food can be sprinkled on the surface of the tank where the food will slowly sink to the bottom. Or it can be mixed with water to form a liquid solution, and then this solution can be fed using an eye dropper. In either case, light aeration should be used to keep the food from settling to the bottom too quickly. Snails are also very useful to help eat any food that was missed by routine tank cleaning.

Powdered foods should be fed at least once a day to older fry to help give them a variety of foods in their diet.

Commercial Fry Foods: On the retail shelves of most pet

shops you will find liquid fry foods that work well. Basically they are foods suspended in a liquid with preservative to keep them from spoiling on the store shelf. They are easy to use and come in handy but they should not be used as the only food for fry. Use them in the same way you would use powdered food.

Gelatin Fry Food: This is a food that will last all day in a fry's tank, thereby giving the fry something to pick at all day long. It should not be used as the only food and the fry have to be at least two to four weeks old before they can eat it.

It's easy to make by dissolving one package of unflavored gelatin in one cup of hot water. Add one bottle each of Gerbers strained egg yolk and strained mixed vegetables. Boil this mixture for one minute. When cooled, it should form a soft-set gel and be soft enough for the fry to eat. For some reason different batches of gelatin will set firmer than others, so do a little testing until the desired results are obtained.

As the fry get older, other ingredients can be added to this mixture to vary the fry's diet. Some other strained baby foods that can be used are chicken, turkey, green vegetables of all kinds, carrots, squash, etc. Make sure all uneaten food is removed daily to prevent water pollution.

Hibernation

We have mentioned earlier that goldfish come from a temperate climate and have adapted to a wide range of temperatures due to climatic changes. It is natural for a goldfish to go through a period of semi-hibernation during the winter, and in fact many goldfish hobbyists believe it is a must for successful goldfish culture. The rigors of the cold hibernation period weed out the weak and unfit, thereby leaving the goldfish hobbyist with stronger, healthier, and more vigorous breeders.

The hobbyist who is breeding a specific line of goldfish will, at times, run into a goldfish who cannot stand the reduced temperatures for a proper hibernation (32° to 45° F). But, as usually happens, the hobbyists will find themselves in the position of

A very nice quality Red Cap Oranda with an excellent cap which does not extend below the eye-line. Red Cap Orandas should have head growth on the top of the head only and not extend to other parts of the head.

having to use this fish as a spawner in order to maintain their line. There is nothing wrong in using this fish for breeding as long as the young from it can go through hibernation. You may want to keep several extra young from this spawn in case some of them have problems during hibernation.

The goldfish hobbyist should try to place his goldfish into hibernation each year. If that is impossible due to climate or a place cold enough in the home or apartment, then a period of reduced food and light during the winter will help your goldfish lose some of that excess fat they have been storing for use during hibernation.

As your goldfish approach the hibernation season, their diet should include increased amounts of carbohydrates. Carbohydrates are easily digested and stored in the goldfish's body which allows them to have ample stored energy to draw from during hibernation.

They need very little extra food during hibernation. In fact all food should be withheld once the water temperature drops below 40° F. When the water is in the 40° to 50° F range a feeding schedule of one to four times a week is more than adequate to maintain the health of the goldfish.

When goldfish are in hibernation, they should be disturbed as little as possible. The hobbyist should examine his goldfish daily, if possible, for signs of disease or swimming difficulty. Swimming difficulty in the form of swim bladder malfunction or poor equilibrium are the biggest problems goldfish have during hibernation. The goldfish having this problem should be removed from the hibernation tank or pond and slowly returned to a warmer temperature where it will usually recover.

Hibernation is a very important part of the goldfish life-cycle. If possible try to give your goldfish a minimum of six to eight weeks of hibernation (below 45° F water temperature). You will be surprised at the increased vigor and appetite they will have after a brief period of hibernation. And the fact that your goldfish has used up most of the stored fat in its system will prevent them from becoming overweight, which is just as harmful to goldfish as it is to people.

So, if possible, reduce your goldfish's water temperature, food and light. This will give you a healthier and more active goldfish which will be around longer to decorate your aquarium and home.

Popular Goldfish

Oranda

This doubletailed breed is one of the most popular and beautiful of all goldfish breeds. The Oranda has a head growth which, in most breeds, covers the whole head. The goose head and redcap Oranda mainly have the growth limited to the top of the head, which forms a high cap. The body of the Oranda is short and round with long flowing fins.

Different fancy varieties of goldfish can be kept together, but it usually is better to group them according to their handicaps. Left to right: a gray Pearlscale, a gold Oranda, and a gold Bubbleye. Photo by Fred Rosenzweig.

Ranchu

This dorsalless breed was developed in Japan. This short, round-bodied fish has a broad head covered with a generous head growth. All of the fins are short with the double tail fin being attached to the caudal peduncle at a sharp angle. The tail fin is held erect and can be fully divided or partially webbed. The curvature along the back is a smooth arch with a sharp angle downward as it nears the caudal peduncle.

A very rare Edonoshiki, Japanese Calico Ranchu, above. Below: Top American strain of Ranchu. Facing page: A good Calico Oranda. Photo by Fred Rosenzweig.

Lionhead

This in another dorsalless breed that has the same general characteristics as the Ranchu. This Chinese breed has much larger head growth and, I think it is safe to say, this breed has the largest head growth of any breed. The short boxy body is propelled by a double tail. View this tail from above and the tail looks like butterfly wings which is very attractive. The back outline is straighter than found in the Ranchu, but it still has a gentle, even curve which is carried right to the caudal peduncle.

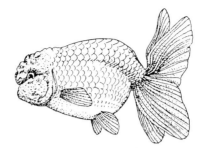

Facing page: A top American strain of Ranchu. Photo by Fred Rosenzweig.

A head-on view of a Chinese Lionhead showing the slope of the back and what appears to be a webbed tail. Photo by Michael Gilroy.

Comet

This truly beautiful American breed is slim and lean and will grace any pond or large aquarium. The single tail fin is as long or longer than the body in high quality fish and each lobe comes to a point. All the other fins of the Comet are much longer than the normal singletailed breeds.

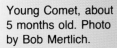

Young Comet, about 5 months old. Photo by Bob Mertlich.

Fantail

The Fantail is the common commercial doubletailed breed of the retail market. Its body is longer than the Oranda but shorter than the singletailed breeds. The head of the Fantail comes to a

106

point and has no head growth. The tail finnage should be long and flowing. More Fantails are sold every year than any other doubletailed breed. They are tough and do equally well in a pond or aquarium. This should be the first doubletailed breed of the beginner as they are very easy to care for.

Shubunkin

There are two types of this singletailed breed. One has a long tail fin with broad tail fin lobes that are rounded on the end. The other has a short tail fin like the common goldfish. What makes these fish a particular breed is that they are of the nacreous scale group (calico) which are primarily bred for their beautiful colors. Red, black, and sky blue are the perfect colors of the calico breeds and the Shubunkins

A common Fantail, the type sold by petshops for the non-dedicated hobbyist. Photo by A. Roth.

A Japanese champion Shubunkin. Photo courtesy of Midori Shobo.

An American Shubunkin. Still a small fish, this 6-month-old male is very promising. Photo by Bob Mertlich.

come closer than any other breed to these ideals. The long bodies are typically fish shaped, like the common goldfish.

Bubble-eye

This is another dorsalless breed, but this breed should have no head growth. This strange breed has a large fluid-filled bubble under each eye that wobbles as the fish swims. The bubbles (from bubble to bubble) can be as wide as the fish is long, which is an awesome sight in a large adult Bubble-eye. The body is long and torpedo shaped with long flowing double tail fins.

A Bubble-eye. Photo by Fred Rosenzweig.

Telescope

This breed has eyes that protrude from the head (globe-eye). The eyes are much larger than found in normal-eyed fish, and the shape can vary from fish to fish. In selecting this doubletailed breed, pay special attention to both eyes, making sure they are the same size and shape. The body of this breed is short and round. This is one of the few breeds where a solid black color over the entire body can be found. This black telescope is called a Moor.

A rare Telescope-eyed Bluescale Fringetail. Some of the scales even look purple. Right: A red and white Broadtail Telescope with very sturdy fins. Photos by Fred Rosenzweig.

Veiltail

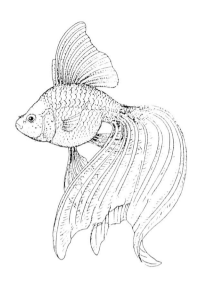

This beautiful round-bodied fish is one of the most exquisite and graceful of the goldfish breeds. Its pointed head has no hood growth. The double tail fins of the Veiltail have no indentation between the lobes. This square cut tail and the very high erect dorsal fin are the features that characterize this breed. The Veiltail finnage can be, and has been, bred into any breed of goldfish. Orandas, Telescopes, Moors, and Pearlscales are all breeds that have had Veiltails bred into them. Veils are not easy to find and are considered to be very rare in the United States.

A rare black and orange Telescope Veiltail. An official description of this fish would be a red and black Broadtail Telescope with caudal, pectoral and dorsal fins in the Veiltail standard. Photo by Fred Rosenzweig.

Pearlscale

This very round-bodied breed has a scale type all its own. In high quality fish each scale has a hard raised area in the center of each scale. This raised area is usually white in color and looks like a half pearl pasted to each scale, thus the name Pearlscale. The double tail fin is square cut like the Veiltail. In the last few years, Pearlscales have been seen with Oranda head growth, long fins and longer bodies. It seems there are a lot of people doing a lot of work with this breed.

Top view of a Pearlscale with well proportioned body, relatively square caudal and pearling all around the back. Photo by Burkhard Kahl.

Champion calico Pearlscale of Chinese heritage. Photo by Fred Rosenzweig.

Celestial

This unique dorsalless breed has a long torpedo-shaped body with long fins. The eyes of the Celestial protrude from the head like they do in the Telescopes, but in the Celestial, the eyes turn to gaze upward at a very early age. The eyes are encased in a hard covering and should be the same size and look in the same direction. The pupils should be the same size also.

The photo above shows a well colored Celestial goldfish. Photo by Klaus Paysan. The photo below shows two English Celestials. Photo by L. Perkins.

Top view of a Pompon.

A well developed pompon goldfish with a full growth of narial bouquets.

Pompon

Another dorsalless breed but this one has a short, round boxy body like a Lionhead with a short double tail fin. The nasal septum (narial flaps) have been enlarged and folded so many times they take on the appearance of velvety peas. Older Pompons will develop a small head growth.

There are several breeds of goldfish that exhibit Pompons. Pompon Orandas, Lionheads and Hanafusa (dorsaled Pompon) are available from time to time. In some of these breeds the Pompons are not much more than ruffled nose flaps (nasal septum) almost covered by head growth, ranging to long, flowing, ruffled streamers with no head growth.

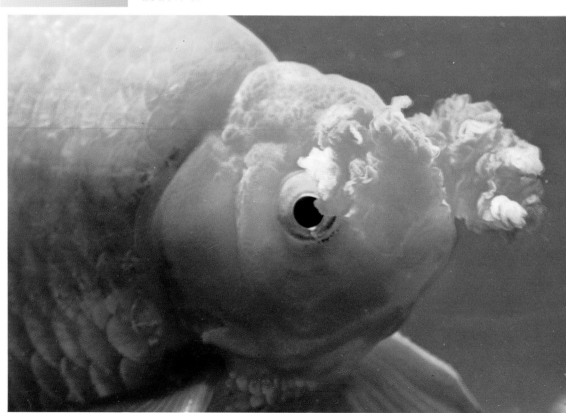

Ryukin

The Ryukin is a very round-bodied goldfish and in the highly developed humpbacked variety it looks like a ball with fins and head attached to it. The Ryukin is one of the most popular goldfish breeds and is a very good breed for the beginner to start with. Ryukins are brightly colored and can be found in red, red and white, white and one of the best calicos of any of the double tailfinned breeds.

Photos courtesy of Midori Shobo.

This is a very high quality Japanese Ryukin with an excellent hump on its back and excellent red markings. This is an older fish and is starting to develop head growth. The hump and head growth are stored fat for winter hibernation. Photo Midori Shobo.

115

Disease

Oh, oh, a sick fish. Even though you believe you have done everything just right and your tank is in perfect order, one of your prized beauties shows all the signs of illness.

Now, before you go and start dumping medication into your aquarium and destroy your undergravel filter and plants, do a little thinking and preparation. First of all, you should try to determine the nature of the illness and if medication is needed. Sometimes a correction or change in the water or environment will correct the problem with no medication at all required.

If the illness is not environment-related, you should isolate the sick fish in a hospital or quarantine tank. By placing it in a separate tank, you will (1) keep the sick fish from infecting its tank mates (2) keep the healthy tank mates from harassing the sick fish (3) use less drugs in treating the disease (4) avoid harming your undergravel filter and plants and (5) it makes it much easier to keep an eye

on the patient for signs of distress.

Your next step should be to try to determine, as accurately as possible, the nature of the illness. In this section we will outline a few of the more common diseases and infections that are the cause of trouble for goldfish.

Fin Congestion

The cause of this problem is an environmental one, such as poor water quality. The long finned breeds are the most susceptible to this problem. Ammonia and organic wastes must be kept to very low levels in fancy goldfish tanks. This illness is easy to recognize by the blood-red areas or blotches on the trailing edges of the fins. Do not confuse the red blood vessels with fin congestion. In fin congestion, there are areas of blood hemorrhages that start at the trailing edge and work their way to the base of the tail.

If caught early, a simple 50% water change will usually clear it up in a few days. If not, give them another 50% water change and add one teaspoon of salt per gallon of water in the nk and enough Methylene lue to turn the water a light .ue. In the vast majority of .ses, this will clear up the n congestion in two or .ree days. If not, and the .ns start to split and fray, .e cause is a bacterial .fection. An antibiotic such : Penicillin or Tetracycline ydrochloride is :commended. Follow the .rections on the package .refully. If the cure is not .mpleted in three days, .ange the water in the tank .d renew the medication. .ost antibiotics break down .ter three days and can .come toxic to the fish.

The surest cure for fin .ngestion is prevention so .ake sure your water quality maintained at all times. .eep the temperature and H level in the mid range .d the ammonia and .itrates very low. The latter particularly important if .e pH is above 7.0.

.h (Ichthyophthirius)

This little parasite is .robably one of the most .mmon afflictions that will other goldfish. It is easy to .iagnose by carefully .xamining your goldfish for .nall white spots. Usually

the fish appears to have been sprinkled with salt which will start in one or two small areas and rapidly spread over most of the body and fins. If treated early it is fairly easy to cure. If allowed to progress, it can be fatal to the fish.

For treatment in the early stages, heat and salt will usually prevent the spread of the parasite. Raise the temperature of the water to 85° F, increase aeration and look for any cause that might have weakened the condition of the fish and correct it, if possible. Ich seldom attacks a healthy fish but will do so immediately if the fish is weakened by some adverse environmental condition. Adding one teaspoon of salt per gallon of water will aid in eliminating the parasites. Treat all of the inhabitants of the tank whether or not they show signs of the infection.

If the infestation is severe, it may be necessary to resort to one of the medications sold for that purpose. Adhere strictly to the manufacturer's directions. Some of these medications will kill the bacteria culture in your undergravel filter as well as the plants and snails (if any) in your tank so it is advisable to remove the plants and snails before the treatment and thoroughly clean the tank and wash or replace the gravel before returning the fish to the tank.

If you are new to the fish-keeping hobby and have never seen "Ich" before, do not panic if you see small white spots on the gill plates or leading edges of the pectoral fins of your male goldfish. These are the breeding tubercles and are normal and will disappear when the fish is no longer in breeding condition.

Velvet

This protozoan parasite is a lot tougher to diagnose. Early infections are almost impossible to see because of the small size of the parasite. As the infection progresses, a fuzzy or dull area will appear on the fish. Unfortunately for the goldfish fancier, this fuzzy area is a golden yellow color and blends in with the normal color of the orange goldfish.

Treatment for Velvet is best left to the commercial products and the directions should be followed to the letter. Many of them contain copper, antibiotics and dyes that, if used in excess, can cause harmful side effects. Heat and progressive salt treatment is effective against Velvet if the disease is diagnosed early enough. A very effective remedy for this, one that is used on tropical fish, is Malachite Green. Goldfish are much more sensitive to Malachite Green than most tropicals and while a quick dip in a relatively strong concentration does not seem to harm them, longer immersions can be fatal in concentrations prescribed for tropicals.

Fungus

This is a fairly easy problem to recognize. Fungus can show up on any part of the fish as an off-white, fuzzy growth. It is usually a secondary infection of an injury and is normally not epidemic in nature. To be safe, remove the fish and treat with the progressive salt treatment (no extra heat), and Methylene Blue painted directly on the fungus. The standard mercurochrome solution can also be used in place of the Methylene blue.

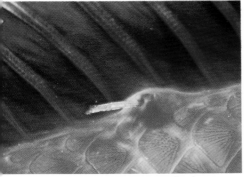

Anchor worm.

The photos on this page depict goldfish parasites (left column) and disease conditions. The adult fish lice and anchor worm are easily visible to the naked eye and require no great degree of magnification to be seen.

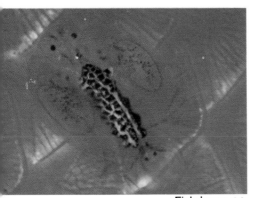

Fish louse on goldfish.

Fin Congestion.

Fish louse.

Fin Congestion.

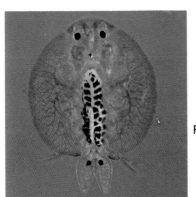

Fish louse.

Photos courtesy of Midori Shobo.

Photos courtesy of
Midori Shobo.

Fungused eggs.

Dropsy.

Body fungus.

COLOR ABNORMALITIES

Amelanotic.

Lutino.

Albino.

Tail rot followed by fungus infection.

Blindness.

alachite Green can also be sed if care is used not to let te fish ingest it.

Body Slime Fungus is a ery virulent type of this isease and if not treated romptly can cause death in vo days. The protective ating of slime on the fish rns white and starts oughing off. The ends of te fins and tail start to fray id slough off as the tfection works up towards te body. Both the body and te fins become red from the ritation. Unfortunately tost antibiotics only stop the eproduction of this fungus id do not kill it. A drastic emedy is required.

A miracle cure for this isease used to be sold under te name of "Tropic Cure." wo 2-second dips in a olution of one tablespoon of 'ropic Cure in 8 ounces of ater killed the fungus and esulted in a complete cure ithin a week. The label sted the ingredients as)24% Merbromin Mercurochrome) and 4% odium Chloride (salt). Iowever, the color of the olution indicated the resence of a copper ompound as well.

If you wish to try making up a similar solution on your own, it is suggested that you start with 4 ounces of a saturated salt solution. To this, add 2 ounces of the standard 2% Tinture of Mercurochrome and one teaspoon of NOX ICH (Malachite Green). Keep this stock solution in a plastic or dark colored bottle. Start by using one teaspoon of the stock solution in eight ounces of water (preferably the same temperature as the aquarium or pond).

Catch the fish in a net and dip the fish in the solution for two seconds. Return it to clean water for five or ten minutes and then give the fish another two-second dip. If the remedy is correct, the fish will come out of the second dip clean and the fins only slightly stained. The fish will suffer no shock and the frayed fins will grow out in a remarkably short time. If the fin does not come out clean, try increasing the strength of the solution (dip) and possibly the length of time in the bath but the former is preferred.

For those who own Orandas and Lionheads with large head growths, you may see what appears to be fungus on the headgrowth during the spring and summer. This is actually new growth and is perfectly normal and will disappear when the weather cools and the fish stops growing. If the appearance bothers you or the growth is cottony and obviously on the surface, apply a drop of Methylene Blue (full strength) on the spots once a day until they no longer return. Shop keepers are famous for diagnosing the very normal head growth condition as a fungus and prescribing various antibiotics for it.

Dropsy

This is actually the symptom of a number of internal bacterial infections. The belly swells and the scales protrude as the condition advances. The Japanese call this the "pine cone" disease. The fish generally lives for a week or more after the condition becomes noticeable. Until recently the condition was considered to be incurable but now some cases have been cured at least temporarily. At the first sighting of a swelling of the abdomen (other than a

female getting "ripe" for spawning), isolate the fish. Put it in a smaller tank with clean water and feed medicated food. Since the infection is internal, the medication must be administered internally.

One other treatment that will work in some cases is to add 250 mg of Furanace in one gallon of water. Put the fish in this bath for one hour and repeat once daily for two more days. Furanace is one of the few medications that can be absorbed through the skin.

Fish that have once had Dropsy are prone to having it again. Clean and disinfect the tank to prevent the other tank mates from coming down with Dropsy also. It does not appear to be contagious, but the condition that caused it in one fish can also cause it in the others.

Injuries

When a fish injures itself, it might be a good idea to isolate the fish to give it time to recover unmolested. One teaspoon of salt to every two gallons of water will promote replacement of the body slime and reduce the chance of infection. Addition of Methylene Blue to the water will also help to reduce the chance of a fungus infection and to keep the fish calm. Keep a close watch on the injury for further complications. At the first sign of secondary infection, treat with an antibiotic.

Parasites

External Parasites: The most prevalent types of external parasites are: Gill Flukes, Skin Flukes, Fish Lice (argulus), Anchor Worms (lernaea) and Leeches. Flukes are so small they can only be seen clearly with a magnifying glass or a microscope. Fish lice are round, flat bugs up to 1/4" long that attach themselves to the fins and body of the fish. Anchor Worms look like short pieces of string projecting from the body or gills of the fish. The head, which is two-pronged, is buried beneath the skin of the fish. Leeches (which are seldom found except in large outdoor ponds) are red, brown or black and can be flat or round and up to 1½" long. They attach themselves to the body of the fish by means of a sucker-like mouth.

The latter three parasites are most commonly controlled by means of a chemical called Dipterex, Masoten, Dylox or Neguvon. Treatment consists of adding enough of this chemical to make a concentration of 0.25–0.40 ppm. It is bio-degradable so no water changes are necessary to remove it after the parasites have been killed. The treatment should be repeated after one week to kill the young parasites that have hatched out after the first treatment. The margin of safety, between the concentration necessary to kill the parasites and that which will kill the fish, is very wide. Excessive use of this chemical can result in crooked backs and other drastic side effects.

Another chemical used by commercial fish farmers is Formalin (37.5% at 25 ppm). The 40% Formalin contains a stabilizing agent that is very toxic to the fish and should not be used for this purpose. The margin of safety is too small for the inexperienced person to try it on his fish.

123

For the aquarium or small pond owners, several companies bottle the Dipterex in standard solutions with simple instructions for its use. The most common of these is Life Bearer, but there are a number of them on the market and all of them are satisfactory. When only a few of the larger parasites are present, they can be removed with a pair of tweezers, and the wound painted with Mercurochrome, Malachite Green or Methylene Blue to prevent infection before it has healed. The Dipterex will also take care of the flukes.

Internal Parasites: There are many types of internal parasites, from round and tapeworms that invade the intestinal tract to others that are microscopic in size, that penetrate the muscles. Any treatment would have to be ingested into the fish and very little work has been done along this line with goldfish or koi. A bath of 250 mg of Furanace in one gallon of water for one hour for three successive days may be of some help but the fish should be isolated to prevent the spread of the infection to other fish.

The tank should also be drained and sterilized with laundry bleach before it is used again. Prevention is the answer and that means careful sanitation and the quarantining of new fish before introducing them into an established tank.

Furunculosis

This bacterial caused disease spreads faster than most diseases the hobbyist will encounter. The early signs of this disease are raised bumps under the scales. In a short time these bumps will rupture, turning into large red ulcers.

To be successful, treatment should be early. Any fish with open ulcers should be destroyed as even if they can be cured (which is in doubt) large scars will be formed. The remaining fish should be treated in their aquarium (goodbye biological filters) with a Tetracycline bath at prescribed levels and a medicated food. Treatment should last 7 to 10 days. Since Furunculosis is a disease of cool water fish, raising the temperature to 80° is beneficial if good water quality can be maintained.

Constipation

This condition is recognized by the swelling of the abdomen and the inactivity of the fish. It usually results from overfeeding of prepared foods that swell as they absorb moisture in the belly of the fish. Isolate the fish, if possible, and add ¼ teaspoon of Epsom salts per gallon of water. Increase the temperature to 80 F. Stop feeding dry and flake food and change to live foods such as Daphnia and Earthworms and green foods such as Duckweed and boiled spinach and zucchini. Do not delay in applying the treatment as constipation will cause swimming bladder problems and result in death for the fish.

After the problem is corrected, change to a smaller size dry food, feed less at each feeding and include one or two of the above foods at least once a week. The shortbodied breeds are most susceptible to this problem—Pearlscales, Ryukins, Tosakins and Veiltails in particular. When feeding pellets, it is a good idea to pre-soak them for a few minutes to allow them to absorb water and swell before feeding them.

Swimming Bladder Problem

This is most common among the short-bodied varieties and usually results from constipation. The swimming bladders vent through the intestines and when the passage is blocked, the fish either float on the surface or sink to the bottom each time they stop swimming. If relief is not obtained within three days, the problem can become permanent. Once afflicted with it, the fish becomes prone to having it happen again and the diet should be changed to a more easily digestible one.

This problem can also be caused by a sudden temperature change, an injury to the swimming bladder, air bubbles forming in the intestines of nacreous fish (especially fry) that have been feeding on algae and are exposed to the bright sun and also from a bacterial infection that causes gas bubbles to form in the intestines. For the latter, an antibiotic such as Furanace must be ingested to be effective.

Appendices

Progressive Salt Treatment

Use non-iodized table salt. This treatment takes 10 days and can be used with or without heat.

Place the fish in a hospital tank that has been filled with clean, aged water. For DAY 1 and 2, add one teaspoon of salt per gallon of water each morning and one teaspoon of salt per gallon each night. If, by DAY 3, there is no improvement, add another teaspoon of salt per gallon in the morning and one teaspoon of salt per gallon at night.

DAY 3, 4, 5, 6, and 7: Observe the fish for improvement. If, by Day 7, no improvement is seen, continue to observe the fish until there is an improvement.

DAY 8, 9 and 10: Remove 50% of the water on each day and replace it with fresh, aged water. This treatment is not a cure-all but it does work well for removing Fungus, Ich, Velvet, Tail Rot and relieving some other problems.

Medicated Food

To every cup of cooled paste food, add 500 milligrams Tetracycline dissolved in a small amount of water. Feed this food for 10 days even if a cure is noticed before the 10 days are up.

Spawning Mops

Artificial material makes a good spawning medium, as it can be easily sterilized with boiling water and can be re-used each year. There are two types that can be used for Goldfish spawning. One is Spawning Grass which is sold in most fish stores. The number of strands that you would need would depend on the size of the fish. The second are Spawning Mops for which you will need synthetic yarn and a cork. They are made quite easily by winding white synthetic yarn around a book. The instructions are as follows: Take a small book about the size of Readers Digest and wind the yarn around the narrow width about 50 times. (A). Next, take a piece of yarn about 12″ long and tie the strands together at the book's binding side. (B). Then cut the strands at

Breeders of certain killifishes (like the pair of *Aphyosemion* shown here) use the same spawning mops recommended in this book. Cork makes them float and a lead wire makes them sink. Lead wires are sold in petshops as 'plant anchors'.

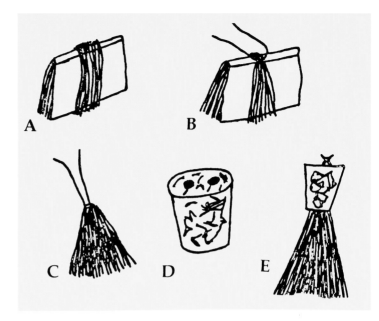

the other end and you have what looks like a long miniature floor mop. (C). Drill two holes lengthwise through the cork. (D). Push the tie strings through the holes and tie them at the top. (E). Your masterpiece should look like the finished product below.

Another method is to use a piece of non-toxic circular wire, put some yarn on it and thereby form a circular pattern mop so the fish can get inside the circle.

NOTE: Boil the new mops before using them the first time. This will remove any harmful chemicals and dyes.

A one year old
Pearlscale and a
Hamanishiki. Photo
by Bob Mertlich.